Seasoned Theatre

A Guide to Creating and Maintaining a Senior Adult Theatre

Martha Haarbauer

ArtAge
Publications

Turn to the
Senior Theatre Resource Center
for your largest collection of
plays, books, materials and
workshops.

PO Box 19955 Portland OR 97280
503-246-3000 or 800-858-4998
Fax: 503-246-3006
bonniev@seniortheatre.com
www.seniortheatre.com

We help mature adults be stars on stage!

This book is dedicated to the talented, courageous,
and committed individuals who are
The Seasoned Performers.
They are my heroes.

Heinemann
A division of Reed Elsevier Inc.
361 Hanover Street
Portsmouth, NH 03801–3912
www.heinemanndrama.com

Offices and agents throughout the world

© 2000 by Martha Haarbauer

Library of Congress Cataloging-in-Publication Data
Haarbauer, Martha.
    Seasoned theatre : a guide to creating and maintaining a senior
adult theatre / Martha Haarbauer.
        p. cm.
    Includes bibliographical references.
    ISBN 0-325-00178-2
    1. Amateur theater. 2. Theater and the aged. 3. Aged—
Recreation. I. Title.
    PN3160.A34 H33 2000
    729'.0222—dc21   99-048514

Editor: Lisa Barnett
Production: Elizabeth Valway
Cover design: Darci Mehall, Aureo Design
Manufacturing: Louise Richardson

Printed in the United States of America on acid-free paper
04 03 02 01 00   DA   1 2 3 4 5

Contents

Foreword

Ann McDonough, Ph.D.

When I was searching for a doctoral thesis topic in 1979, my advisor, Dr. Kenneth L. Graham at the University of Minnesota, suggested that I write about "this new thing called senior adult theatre." I recall asking him what it was, and he responded excitedly that it was theatre by, with, and for older adults. "Theatre that expresses the aging experience."

Dr. Graham went on to exclaim that senior adult theatre would be the next major movement in the story and practice of the art of the theatre. Indeed, he was prophetic. There are now approximately eighty-eight performing companies in the United States, and the study of senior adult theatre is quickly becoming formalized. In my program at the University of Nevada–Las Vegas, for instance, we are offering the first bachelor of arts in senior adult theatre. Students of a variety of ages over eighteen years are learning to teach theatre to older adults, direct older actors, write plays for senior adult theatre, and start senior adult theatre companies.

It is inspiring and exciting to see the number and types of companies and educational programs that have developed in the twenty years that have passed since Dr. Graham urged me to go into senior adult theatre. In Columbus, Ohio, for instance, Grandparents Living Theatre has thrived for more than ten years, performing all over the United States and in Europe. In Fresno, California, The New Wrinkles, affiliated with Fresno City College, packs in audiences for performances of its delightful reviews, and in Chicago, Illinois, Northlight Theatre's senior adult theatre company and program has attracted widespread acclaim.

This growth of senior adult theatre from coast to coast has mirrored the enormous growth in the ranks of senior adults. As these ranks have grown, theatre teachers and professionals, as well as professionals at all levels of aging services, have recognized the need for senior adult theatre. The challenge for many of these people is that they do not know where to begin in terms of starting a company and/or program, because the field is so new and formal training is not readily available at this point. In fact, it is not unusual for me to receive requests for guidance on the business of starting a senior adult theatre project and choosing the best dramatic materials.

Thus, Martha Haarbauer's book is making a much-anticipated entrance! It is with great pleasure that I will now be able to direct people seeking to start a senior adult theatre program or company to this comprehensive text on creating and maintaining a company. Ms. Haarbauer's hands-on experience in managing The Seasoned Performers will be a valuable guide in a variety of important areas such as organizing, funding, understanding the unique needs and conditions of older adults, and managing the office.

This book is unique in that it ably covers the business of senior adult theatre. There are useful anthologies of dramatic literature for older adults on the market as well as texts on Creative Drama for senior adults and a text that I have written on teaching acting to older adults. *Seasoned Theatre: A Guide to Creating and Maintaining a*

Senior Adult Theatre is the first work, however, that offers comprehensive, practical direction on the nuts and bolts of starting a company. It will be the compass that guides you on what I hope will be an exciting adventure.

It is not always easy to view the process of starting a senior adult theatre program as an exciting adventure. Often it takes courage and repeated requests for help and money from academic institutions and community agencies. This guide, however, will be a valuable companion and will support you as you create your company. Indeed, I would say to you what a wise professor told me ten years ago as I was struggling to develop the senior adult theatre program at the University of Nevada–Las Vegas: "Just get out there and do it." I say to you, "Just get out there and do it, but take this valuable book with you on your journey!"

Preface

A new stage.

In the theatre, this can be inviting and exhilarating when the possibilities of stories, characters, action, dialogue, and ideas are infinite and just waiting to be selected—or it can be empty, bleak, and frightening when no inspiration comes. In life, the same is true, especially when the new stage is "modern maturity," the retirement years, senior adulthood, or whatever label one might choose. Of course some don't wish to label the years beyond . . . a certain age . . . anything but *life*, and perhaps this is best. In any case, to carry on our theatre analogy, the term *new stage* for these years seems preferable to *the final act!*

Indeed, this new stage of life has brought into being a vital new act in the arena of theatre—a new stage that gives consideration to the needs, interests, abilities, and disabilities of its older participants and audiences. Senior adult theatres have emerged individually and collectively as energetic, challenging, and artistically satisfying ventures.

This book is about creating and maintaining a senior adult theatre. It gives information, resources, and examples and offers ideas and suggestions based primarily on lessons learned in the fifteen-year history of one specific senior adult theatre—The Seasoned Performers. (Perhaps *seasoned* is the most accurate and palatable term of all.) It is hoped that *Seasoned Theatre* will be helpful to those thinking of starting such a theatre; to already-established organizations interested in developing and sustaining their program; and to theatre professionals who wish to explore the possibilities of this kind of theatre work. The book will cover aspects such as organizing a senior adult theatre, finding and working with the special actors, choosing material, making technical decisions, and locating the place to work, the audiences, and the money. It presents a broad range of possibilities to help you make decisions based on your current circumstances and make plans for the future development of your group.

The book doesn't try to teach the art of theatre. There are many books on that subject, and it is best to have a knowledgeable leader or consultant for a senior adult theatre project of any scope. Whether you are starting a small drama group within a retirement community or church, creating a special wing to an already-established community or university theatre, or starting an independent, fully self-supporting entity, this book offers recommendations and guidance in the business of senior adult theatre.

Acknowledgments

My sincere gratitude to:

Ward Haarbauer, whose wise suggestions—not to mention proofreading—helped shape and complete this book;

Eric Haarbauer, without whose computer knowledge this book and many Seasoned Performers accomplishments would not have been made;

Terrell Knight and Avanelle Weldon of The Seasoned Performers, whose loyalty, dedication, and service beyond the call of reasonable duty have sustained so many theatre projects;

Linda Vice and Mary Bess Price of the Jefferson County Office of Senior Citizens Services, for continued support and assistance in the areas of organization and funding—and cheerleading;

Irene Collins and Brian Davis of the Jefferson County Council on Aging, for essential information in the areas of nonprofit organizations;

Becky Mullen of the Alabama State Council on the Arts, for her guidance pertaining to arts councils and grant writing;

Dr. Ann McDonough of the University of Nevada–Las Vegas, for her research and work with senior adult theatre—and for sharing it with so many;

Dolores Hydock, founder and director of the Kirkwood Accomplished Thespian Society, for her insight in working with seniors in retirement centers;

Lang Reynolds of the Department of Theatre, University of Alabama at Birmingham, for technical consultation;

Terri Kohl, director of The Merry Clements Players in Lakewood, Colorado, who shared information on resources;

Sarah Worthington of Footsteps of the Elders in Columbus, Ohio, whose connections led to many good resources;

Bill and Evie Weddel of the Slightly Older Adult Players (SOAP) in Fort Collins, Colorado, who allowed the troupe's bylaws to be used as a sample in Appendix IV;

Don Drapeau, of Virginia Tech, who led me to this publisher; and

Barbara Bonfield, whose commitment and vision resulted in a senior adult theatre in Birmingham, Alabama.

A Personal Word

When the director of the local area agency on aging called me in the spring of 1984 and asked me to lead an acting workshop for a group of senior citizens who wanted to do a play, I thought I was prepared. I had been teaching acting for ten years, especially to the nontheatre majors, at the University of Alabama at Birmingham. So I had experience with students new to the craft. I had worked in many capacities in the theatre, including designing costumes and setting up and managing the first costume shop for the university's theatre department. I had a degree in theatre from the University of Alabama and had worked in many shows, including some professional summer work in North Carolina. However, I had no idea what I was about to get into.

Somehow, by the fall of that year I was the project director of the same troupe, which we renamed The Seasoned Performers. I knew that there was real potential here—that there were senior adult groups all over the county and beyond and that these groups were growing and looking for entertainment and stimulating ideas. I knew that I had a group of people—all women—who were committed to giving their best to this activity and that I had total moral support from the area agency on aging. I knew that here was an opportunity to get paid for doing theatre without having to compete with the mainstream theatres in the area. And I knew that we would not be judged by the same standards.

Little did I know that one day we could hold our own

with the best of them, or that we would indeed be competing for some of the same funding as other local theatres, or that I would have to become a fund-raiser—and a troubleshooter! I didn't know that I would learn so much or have so many new windows on life opened for me—or that I would become so inspired by the participants that I would be in total awe of them.

Lack of budget and lack of material were our first two hurdles. We learned, first of all, how much we could actually do with nothing—or with minute amounts of money and lots of in-kind support. And then we learned that a long life is a vast resource for theatre material.

We mined the memory banks of the small core of original Seasoned Performers to discover precious metal—stories, experiences, events—and we made theatre. We had stories from our vaudevillian tap dancer from New York, dirt farmers from rural Alabama, a waiter in Birmingham, a caregiver, and an FBI agent. We didn't know we were doing oral histories, today a respected genre in senior adult theatre. We were just using what we had, and it worked.

I had to be pushed into attempting to write the first grant proposal in 1986. That wasn't why I went into theatre! Necessity is the mother of some lessons. It was the first real step forward into the phenomenal growth of the theatre program.

Sixteen original plays, several vans, a new performance wing, and thousands of miles later, we would all say it's been quite a trip. And the best part of the trip is ahead of us. There is still such incredible potential for The Seasoned Performers senior adult touring theatre.

I wish I'd had a book like this to guide us when we began, but then that might have made it too easy—or I might have been overwhelmed and given up. As a matter of fact, there have been times when I've wanted to give up. I'm glad I didn't and I hope you don't. Leading a senior adult theatre can be grueling and frustrating, but the rewards can be much greater.

Remember, even The Seasoned Performers players haven't always followed all the guidelines in this book, and the theatre has survived. We've always tried to do what we could do at the time and we've done it our way. We've developed step by step. We succeeded in large measure because (1) there was a need for the program, (2) we've had several key people willing and able to go beyond the call of duty for the theatre, (3) we've made some important community contacts in the arts, funding agencies, and corporations, and (4) the program has a degree of flexibility, with the ability to change when necessary.

The Seasoned Performers troupe is still evolving. We are currently in the process of making a long-range plan that will probably change the programming somewhat over the next five years. This is to fill our changing needs and those of the community. The prospects are exciting.

I plan to start phasing out as director within that time frame. Will I retire to start volunteering with The Seasoned Performers? Absolutely. What's my cue?

Introduction

The Seasoned Performers senior adult touring theatre is based in Birmingham, Alabama, and is still inventing itself after fifteen years of productive life and energetic growth. Starting in 1984 with an operating budget of approximately $7,000 a year, the theatre now has an annual budget of almost $70,000, including in-kind services. The Seasoned Performers troupe tours a newly commissioned one-act play or theatre piece each year to more than sixty-five different sites reaching older audiences in retirement facilities, churches, libraries, and community centers and younger audiences in schools. Occasionally, these troupers even perform in a theatre!

Each play is double cast and the two casts alternate performances four mornings a week for two months each spring and another two months every fall, filling in for each other when necessary. The split schedule allows the theatre to take its play to the many different sites on the circuit, touring when the weather is the most pleasant and the demand is the highest and giving the actors a rest between jaunts. Their tours are usually within the home county, but they also reach up to ten nearby counties each year. These actors are all volunteers and range in age from around fifty to about eighty-seven actively creative years.

The Seasoned Performers program also has another performing wing called The Seasoned Readers, which develops its own reading programs of poetry, stories, and readers theatre pieces for touring to small audiences in an additional forty community sites. This wing was recently begun in order to fill different kinds of needs of both the participants and the audiences.

The program sponsors theatre workshops of various sorts for older adults in the community as well as occasional "seeing theatre" ventures for its participants. Future plans include a series of matinees in collaboration with a local community theatre.

The theatre works year-round to live up to its mission of (1) providing opportunities for older adults to participate in theatre arts, (2) bringing quality, live theatre to audiences of older adults and students, and (3) providing a training base for older adults who wish to grow in theatre skills and knowledge. The theatre also remembers its original mandate from its founders to use theatre to dispel the myths of aging and bring a positive image of older adults to the general population.

The Seasoned Performers theatre is under the auspices of a larger nonprofit organization that oversees a number of services to the elderly in the area. The director of the theatre is contracted separately through the local area agency on aging, an office that offers various programs and assistance for the elderly.

All of the support money beyond the director's contract is raised each year by the theatre and represents a variety of sources, including granting agencies, government support, individual and corporate donations, performance fees, and special fund-raising activities. In-kind support includes rehearsal space donated by a local church and bookkeeping provided by the umbrella service organization.

The Seasoned Performers troupe has performed in Washington, D.C., for the National Association of Area Agencies on Aging, and at the Southeastern Theatre Conference when it met in Birmingham, Alabama. The troupe has been a finalist in Birmingham's Mayor's Awards for the arts, and the director was presented a Silver Bowl Award by Birmingham's Festival of Arts for her work with the senior adult group. The Seasoned Readers group has performed for the Governor's Arts Awards in Montgomery, Alabama.

The theatre did not originate with its current programming and budget. It has grown in small and large steps along its fifteen-year history. It has experimented with many types of performance material and workshop themes, tried an assortment of performance venues and working spaces, used different scheduling, and raised money from a variety of sources. It has had a great deal of success and over its lifetime has also faced failures that have brought with them valuable lessons.

Although The Seasoned Performers troupe represents a very unique type of theatre, there are elements of organization, maintenance, and programming that can apply to any senior adult theatre. The fact that this theatre has not only survived but is still growing in every way says something about its solid structure, the spirit and tenacity of its participants, and the need for such a theatre in its community.

1

Organizing

Being excited and enthusiastic about the prospect of creating a theatre group is one thing. The prospect of sorting through the options and making your way through seemingly endless requirements and long processes can be quite another. Becoming a viable entity that is operational and ongoing takes a real commitment as well as time and careful planning. Perhaps you will want to try several productions to test the waters and build interest before you decide what kind of organization you ultimately want to become.

There is a range of choices of structure that a senior adult theatre can take. Your program may be a very informal group within a retirement community, a program associated with a larger organization such as a senior center, or perhaps the goal is to build a larger, more complex, self-sustaining entity. Some of the possibilities and procedures are described here.

A Mission Statement

What special needs do you want to fill? Each organization has to answer this question for itself, and each answer will be unique depending on the community, the individuals involved, experience, resources, size, preferences, and so on. The answer to this question need not be complete at first. As a matter of fact, it is a good thing to leave room for changes, development, and growth. But in order to decide upon the best plan and to set immediate and long-range goals, it is wise to get a clearly written statement of your group's goals and designated constituencies. After your overall mission statement is defined, you can list the more specific activities and services that you want to provide. For an example of a mission statement, see the Introduction (2).

What needs do you see in your particular community that are not being served? Do you see older actors dropping out of community theatre because of the unrelenting demands on their physical and emotional energy? Do you see a smaller and smaller older audience because of physical limitations or because the theatre today has left it behind? Are there defined groups who need stimulating, live theatrical entertainment? Do you see talented theatre professionals lacking in employment due to scarcity of places to work? Do you see numbers of older people who would like to participate in theatre activities but who never had the time before or who lack the experience—or the nerve—to compete with other actors? Are there older people who need more opportunities for daytime activity? These are good reasons to create something new that can fill these needs.

In writing your mission statement, it is good common sense to consider not only the *needs of your community* but also the *special focuses of funding sources*. You can readily identify arts granting agencies; corporations with a vested interest in the elderly such as banks and investment establishments, utilities, drug companies, etc.; local agencies that assist the elderly; retirement facilities; and other places where you are likely to find an audience—and ask! What needs would they like such a group to meet? Perhaps you can incorporate their desires into your mission and thus make it easier to find funding and other support for your project. Not all senior adult theatres will be qualified for funding from some of these sources. Check the printed guidelines of granting agencies or ask representatives of funding sources for information about eligibility.

Listen to everyone, sort through the information, and make your statement as broad as you can while still giving your project a unique goal and place in the community and in the ranks of all the others competing for the same money. Don't overlook the possibility of including some form of education and outreach in your mission statement. If you can incorporate these goals into your program, your recruitment and fund-raising potentials go up. Arts granting agencies like to support projects that generate new participants as well as new patrons of the arts.

It may become clear by defining your mission that some organization is already in place with parallel goals. In this case it may be best to join forces and perhaps become a special part of that group. For instance, a community theatre with some older audience members may be interested in developing a senior theatre wing in order to better serve and expand that segment of its audience and to attract older actors. A community center for older adult activities and services may have space and other support to offer a theatre group. Partnerships offer strengths and resources and often simplify organizational processes that can use up precious time and energy.

Look around your community first. If you decide that forming a new theatre is best for your goals and your community, then pursue your vision!

Nonprofit Status

The primary reasons for a theatre to be classified as non-profit are to be exempt from certain taxes and to be eligible to receive grants from various charitable and arts funding agencies that require this status from all recipients of their funding. Also, individuals who contribute to a 501(c)(3) organization can, with certain limitations, take a charitable contribution deduction from their federal income tax return.

A 501(c)(3) organization is a nonprofit organization that meets the requirements of section 501(c)(3) of the Internal Revenue code and has been recognized by the IRS as exempt from certain federal income taxes and other taxes designated by this section. Any nonprofit organization needs to establish itself as a legal entity under state law before seeking recognition as a 501(c)(3) organization. This entity is usually a *corporation*, which necessitates creating a business plan and filing the organization's articles of incorporation and bylaws with the state in which the corporation will operate. After this process, you can complete Federal Tax Form 1023 to apply for recognition by the IRS. If applicable in your state, a request for a state exemption can also be made. Appendix IV of this book contains sample bylaws of a nonprofit theatre.

More information on these procedures and legalities for establishing nonprofit organizations can be found in books or on the Internet and requested from arts councils or government sources. Be as knowledgeable as you can, but the fact is, you will probably want the services of a good lawyer who is well acquainted with the complex laws concerning nonprofit organizations. Not all lawyers are. Try to get recommendations from other local nonprofit organizations and select your counsel carefully. Getting set up properly in the first place can save money, time, and headaches later. The process does take time, but you can operate while this is being done.

Although the expenses—and pressures—may be greater for an individual nonprofit organization than one that is "under the auspices of" another nonprofit organization, it is to your advantage in several ways to have your own classification. This gives a greater power of decision making to people who are directly concerned with the theatre (your board), reduces the number of offices and/or people any one transaction and communication has to go through, simplifies a number of processes, guarantees that you are not competing with other areas of your organization for the same money, and assures that all efforts are for the direct benefit of your theatre's goals and needs.

Stagebridge, the oldest senior adult theatre in the nation, is an example of a nonprofit senior theatre company. Located in Oakland, California, this theatre actively serves its mission of making theatre an opportunity for older people and of using theatre to bridge the generations. Actually beginning as a drama class at an Oakland senior center in 1978, the group formed the College Avenue Players and began seeking support from local corporations and foundations. By 1985, the company had grown in both programming and support and it officially incorporated. Later changing its name to more clearly suggest the company's work in spanning generations, the theatre now operates five separate programming areas and receives support from a wide array of sponsors including national and local arts and government agencies and corporations. (Programming information on this and other companies appears in Chapter Four. Contact information is in Appendix II.)

An independent, nonprofit theatre troupe with a different specific focus is Footsteps of the Elders in Columbus, Ohio. This small troupe is made up of older women who, since 1994, have worked with improvisations—theatrical scenes with no written script in which performers create the lines—based on their own reminiscences. This company, which has toured internationally, offers its oral histories to presenters who pay a performance fee and expenses for the touring company. Other support comes from small grants and even bartered goods and services. The group may give a performance for the use of rehearsal space, for instance.

Cooperative efforts can help fill the needs of a community. The SOAP Troupe, an acronym for Slightly Older Adult Players, operates with cooperation and support from the Fort Collins Senior Center, although the theatre is a nonprofit organization with its own 501(c)(3) classification. SOAP has a written agreement with the city of Fort Collins, Colorado, Parks and Recreation Adult Program that outlines the roles of the city and the theatre troupe in accomplishing the goals of the program. A member of the senior center staff is included on the SOAP Troupe board. While the theatre charges a membership fee and earns money from ticket sales, it can receive contributions from various other sources. Also, an organization called Friends of the Senior Center helps in generating funds for some of the troupe's special projects. A percentage of some performance proceeds are given back to the senior center in return for its support.

Alliances with Established Organizations

There are, on the side of legal alliances, a number of benefits to be reaped from these associations. If your theatre can be a separate project under the umbrella of an established nonprofit or other organization that serves a similar constituency or has parallel goals, then you may be wise to explore the possibilities and negotiate a workable agreement.

The process of becoming officially recognized by the

Internal Revenue Service as a nonprofit 501(c)(3) organization can be daunting and long. A link with an already-established structure can simplify your life by eliminating this step and will qualify your theatre for funding under the name and classification of the larger organization.

An umbrella organization can provide insurance and health and pension benefits for staff. There can be other perks such as sharing of office space, staff, and equipment and locating of funding sources in return for your artistic efforts, but these matters must be agreed upon specifically in advance and in writing.

In the case of The Seasoned Performers, the theatre is one of a number of different services to the elderly that are overseen by its umbrella nonprofit organization. A board of directors and an executive director work with an office staff to assure that all the programs perform their missions and comply with the federal regulations that apply to all nonprofit organizations. The Seasoned Performers raises its budget separately, but the bookkeeping is done by the overseeing body. An accounting firm does the required outside audit and financial statement each year for the entire organization. The Seasoned Performers has its own space and staff but works with the overseeing association's staff in bookkeeping, money handling and records, and certain documentation—everything that pertains to operating legalities.

Universities and colleges are interested in senior adults as prospective students and donors, of course, but also as a specific segment of a broader community with which these institutions wish to connect and service in various ways. A number of these schools already have very active senior adult theatre and entertainment groups connected within their systems. A tremendous advantage to this alliance is the possible availability of the school's faculty, staff, equip-

11

ment, and facilities. The senior adult theatre can draw attention to the university's programs, and interactions between generations can be an educational bonus.

The Extended Run Players, established in 1996, is supported by the University of the Incarnate Word in San Antonio, Texas. This group is a voluntary association of senior members presenting readers theatre productions on campus and in the community. Their proceeds are used for theatre scholarships at the university. The university staff manages the company and organizes meetings and performances. Student volunteers sometimes assist with productions to the mutual benefit of both the older players and young students.

There are other places in the community where a senior adult theatre might naturally fit into the established structure, such as parks and recreation boards, retirement facilities, large churches, continuing education organizations, and community theatres.

The award-winning Merry Clements Players operates through the Clements Community Center of the city of Lakewood in Colorado. The director of this group is contracted by the city of Lakewood to work with seniors in the community center, where the troupe is given space to rehearse. Their productions earn fees by touring to senior adult groups and schools in the Denver area. The profits from a large fund-raising production at the center each year is split between the theatre program and the community center.

One of the simplest organizations is a troupe called the Kirkwood Accomplished Thespian Society (KATS), located in a retirement community near Birmingham, Alabama, called Kirkwood By The River. A local actress and storyteller has volunteered for the last ten years as the group's director, leading monthly sessions of drama activity that occasionally result in simple productions by the small group of residents. While some retirement centers may be able to offer funding for such a project, this group operates with no budget other than some office support and exemplifies one extreme of the wide range of existing senior adult theatres.

There are growing populations of older adults in most communities, and organizations are looking for ways to serve them. If an organization wants a senior adult theatre, it can work with you to find ways to make a start on the budget, offer facilities and other support, and help in recruiting participants.

Before you go into such an alliance, it is important to know not only what kinds of support you will be given but what financial assistance you will be eligible for from other areas such as arts or senior adult granting agencies and city, state, and county agencies, as well as other community sources. Will you be competing for the same money? Will you be ineligible to apply for certain grants because of your association with the larger organization? The more broad-based your financial support, the easier to find your budget each year. Granting agencies are very specific about who is eligible to apply for funding, and you may want to design your theatre to fit their criteria. Check with your state arts council and your local area agency on aging. These can be invaluable sources of guidance and information.

Boards, Advisory Committees, and Friends

The rules for nonprofit corporations are very specific about establishing a board of directors to oversee the policies and operations of the organization. Many states require at least three directors, but often these boards are much larger. The bylaws of the organization will define methods of electing these board members. In the sample bylaws in Appendix IV, the officers are given duties that cover much of the actual work of running the company. Most organizations want people on their board who are well established in the community, who have specific appropriate areas of experience and expertise, and who have other contacts who can be called upon for various needs and reasons. The members of these boards take on legal responsibility for the proper actions of the organization, so it is important that they be committed and active even if a staff does most of the work.

In choosing a board for a senior adult theatre group, it may be helpful to look for people with a genuine interest in the arts who also have specific helpful knowledge or experience with the following areas:

1. theatre
2. law
3. other nonprofit organizations
4. fund-raising
5. older adults
6. the corporate community
7. public relations and marketing
8. education
9. affluent society

Strong leadership and commitment is necessary, especially from the officers, for a board to function properly and actively. The board members should work well with all staff of the theatre to make sure that legalities are met, that the organization is fulfilling its mission, that programming is running smoothly, that proper and creative planning is being done, and that the organization is finding the necessary resources to function and grow. The board should establish ways in which it can be actively helpful in areas of need.

Local arts councils can offer guidance in developing a board as well as in other areas of starting your program. Some offer periodic workshops in these and other areas. These are often helpful not only in the specific workshop topic but in making contacts and learning about other arts groups and how they work. Other small arts groups can also be a source of advice and are often more inclined than large ones to share knowledge and form alliances.

Advisory committees are not legally responsible for the workings of an arts group but can be most helpful in guiding the director, staff, and participants in planning, programming, fund-raising, and so on. This type of group is especially needed when your theatre is under the auspices of a larger organization whose board is focused on the proper functioning and legalities of the broader whole and not on the specific programming, fund-raising, etc. of the theatre. An advisory committee can focus more specifically and intimately on the needs and goals of your theatre without the distraction of the larger responsibility.

An advisory committee should be made up in general like a board of directors, with members having various fields of expertise and reasons to be devoted to your cause. Its members should have real experience in areas in which you are working so that they can indeed advise with knowledge and experience and not just form an opinion from the heart. Members of an advisory committee may decide that they are there to advise, not to do any of the active work, although they can agree to be more actively involved.

Without the legal responsibilities applicable to a board, an advisory committee can be organized as formally or loosely as the individuals want. Depending upon the size and special needs of the program, this support group can be any size and can function as generally or as specifically as warranted. Regular meetings should be held in which committee members are brought up to date on all projects. Small focus groups within the committee may be created so that individuals can take more responsibility in advising or helping in areas in which they are most qualified and interested. These areas may include (1) programming and performance material, (2) finances and fund-raising, (3) marketing and audience development, (4) recruitment and support of volunteer performers and other participants, (5) workshops and other activities, and (6) management and office procedures.

"Friends" of an arts organization usually come together to help in raising money for a group. Although these friends sometimes offer hands-on help in a production or in project organization, their involvement does not involve legal support or advice but supports the efforts of the arts group. An annual or semiannual fund-raiser organized by friends can free up the artists to focus on their creative endeavors without draining their energy in other directions. Whereas friends of a young ballet troupe or children's theatre often involve the parents who have a vested interest in the group, friends of a senior adult theatre may involve the children of the performers!

Staff

In many successful community theatres there is no paid staff, but seasons of plays actually do get produced. There are people who want to do theatre so much that they are willing to do what it takes to make it happen. People of all ages have such energy and passion for the theatre that they are willing to do the work for no compensation except the love of doing it and perhaps a little applause. However, even in theatres such as these, it is much easier to find good performers, directors, and even technicians than it is to find the people who will raise the money, plan the seasons, organize the mailings, do the printing, sell the tickets, write the press releases, manage the house, and so on. Regardless of whether there is a paid staff, there must be an organized group of people willing and able to handle the necessary jobs. This may fall to the board of the theatre, to volunteers, or to a staff.

The Seasoned Performers started with one paid, part-time staff member who did everything, including occasionally standing in as an actor. Now there are three regular part-time staff members including a project director, a technician, and a tour manager/clerical associate. Other artists such as directors, workshop leaders, writers, and technical assistants are hired for special short-term services. With this paid assistance, The Seasoned Performers program is able to operate all year with workshops and touring. The basic workload of producing ongoing and seasonal performance and learning opportunities for the participants, producing shows, and getting them to special audiences includes

1. organizing grant administration and other fund-raising
2. creating budgets
3. keeping financial and statistical records and reporting them
4. commissioning and producing a new script each year
5. organizing other performance material
6. producing workshops and scheduling rehearsals
7. marketing the shows and performing other public relations duties
8. designing the productions
9. overseeing all technical production of the shows

10. managing the tours
11. accompanying the tours
12. running the shows
13. overseeing the office
14. supervising space and storage
15. recruiting and organizing the volunteers

Whatever the scope of a theatre's programming and regardless of whether there are paid staff, there are usually many details for which someone has to be responsible. In general, for a full theatre program, the areas of management, artistic direction, and technical direction must have committed coverage before the work can begin.

Older actors need this support to be especially strong and dependable. The best way to make sure that this kind of support is available usually is to have paid staff at some level. The chances of continuation and development of the theatre are better if a solid funding source can be found for *at least* one well-qualified part-time staff member. When this is not possible, an organized structure should be in place with people who agree to handle the specific jobs.

Business Plans

Even if you are thinking of starting a less formal theatre group, it is advisable to start with a simple business plan. The same kind of planning that goes into the more complex organizations can help to assure your group of an operating mechanism that will work.

Begin by defining your mission and goals, then decide what activities you want to do. What people will your group serve? How will the organization fit into the community and what will be its unique contribution?

Plan how your activities will be financed. Knowing

what the funding sources are and understanding what it will take to raise the money is basic in preliminary planning. At this point, making the first several years' budgets will help clarify financial goals. (See Chapter Two for more on planning budgets and finding the funding.)

Who will operate your theatre? What will their responsibilities be? This includes volunteers, staff, board, and advisors. Where will you find and recruit them?

The answers to these questions will not only help define the operations but will also help in making decisions about the type of organization needed. Try to be realistic as well as optimistic.

. . .

Every theatre has to begin somewhere. Don't be discouraged if you can't have it all in the beginning. It will be better to limit production plans at first until you can gradually obtain more of the basic necessities—or the money with which to buy them. You may wish to keep your senior adult theatre program very simple, but a few tenacious people can make surprising things happen over time.

2

Funding

After deciding what kind of organization your theatre will have and what will be its mission and goals, there follows the process of making a business plan to implement these goals. This will include creating budgets and researching ways to finance them. Once you know how much money the theatre needs and what funding resources are available to your group, planning can begin for a fund-raising campaign. By and large, this process is no different for a senior adult theatre than any theatre except that there may be a slight difference in some specific budgeting needs and in some of the funding sources.

How Much Will It Cost?

From "homemade" plays done in the backyard to the most spectacular productions on Broadway, people have created engaging theatre on budgets of all sizes. Whether you are starting on a very small budget, as The Seasoned Performers did in 1984, or have the prospect of starting with much healthier funding, the first consideration in planning for the monetary support of your theatre is estimating how much money it will take to fulfill your goals. Then you can begin to explore the possible sources for this money.

In the planning stages of your organization it will be helpful to gather all the information you can about the real cost of the necessary components of your plan. This will not only help in creating the budget, but this hard information will help you in *raising* the funds and in *planning* for the future of your theatre.

In the beginning there may be certain start-up costs, such as equipment and consultants' fees, that will not be as great in successive years. Planning budgets and programming goals for several years at a time is good management and will continue to be helpful in encouraging your theatre to grow.

There is no one model of a budget, since there are so many varieties and sizes of senior adult theatres, but the following budget categories could be included in running a theatre organization:

- administrative and artistic personnel (these items include any full- or part-time staff salaries)
- outside fees (these may include artistic and technical assistance; legal and other consultants; and an outside audit)
- employee benefits (medical; social security; etc.)
- production (royalties; settings; sound; lighting; costumes; properties; printing; etc.)
- marketing (direct mailings and other advertising; printing; postage; etc.)
- transportation (vehicle rental or repairs; gasoline; mileage; etc.)
- insurance (general liability; workman's compensation; any vehicle insurance; other liabilities specified by the organization as directors' and officers'; professional; etc.)
- space (rehearsal, office, and storage rental; utilities; etc.)
- supplies (office; rehearsal; workshops; etc.)
- telephone service
- maintenance
- volunteer support (this may include training; gifts; lunches; mileage; social events; etc.)
- equipment (office and production)

- development (seminars and other training; literature; consultants; may also include new projects and fund-raisers)
- contingency fund (emergencies or unexpected opportunities)

Budgeting the time to do the initial research for your theatre's budget is crucial. You should have a realistic idea of what your costs will be to start and run the theatre project. This includes going into the marketplace and pricing items, interviewing individuals who are doing similar projects or who may be working for you, talking with vendors, reading catalogs, etc. and finding all the facts and information you can. Even if you think you will be getting in-kind support in some areas, knowing the actual cost of these items will be of value in writing proposals for funding.

Your budget estimates should include both actual cash demands and in-kind costs of services and goods. These in-kind items may include donated space; administrative costs if your project is overseen by a larger organization; consulting time donated by professionals; free advertising or other services such as printing; loans of production necessities such as equipment or properties, etc. Including these in budget proposals is important because funding agencies want to know the actual total cost of your project and what kinds of other support you have, and these costs will count as matching funds for certain grants. You may choose to include an in-kind estimate for talent in your budget when your actors and crew are volunteers. When you multiply the number of hours put into a production by a reasonable price per hour, this figure totals quite a sum!

Where Will the Money Come From?

The very best situation would be an endowment, which

would earn an annual income in perpetuity to cover at least a part of each year's budget. This would require a very large sum from a benefactor or support system but would reduce the struggle to raise the whole budget each year. Even if you have this kind of support, however, it is likely that you will need to do some form of fund-raising to reach your goals. In this case, your theatre will be healthier and more able to weather crises of various kinds if you have a broad base of funding. Once you secure a few sources it may become easier to find others.

The process of seeking funding is an ongoing one. As you acquire a track record of good work and become better known in the community, your fund-raising potential will grow. It may, however, take a number of years to be recognized as a viable entity in the community in order to attract grants and donations. It may also take a period of time to discover sources for which your organization is eligible and to learn which means of fund-raising are the most effective for meeting your particular needs.

Funding Sources

Earned Income
In theatre, a product is usually created that is expected to "sell" to audiences. This earned income for a senior adult theatre may be season ticket or individual ticket sales, performance fees, workshop fees, sales of program advertising, and concession sales. Interest on bank accounts can also be termed earned income. As in most nonprofit theatres around the country, this earned income will probably not net enough to support a healthy program. This is especially true in serving senior adult and other special audiences when it is advisable to keep ticket and other prices relatively low.

In estimating the income from these sources it will be

23

necessary to know how many performances you will do, the seating capacity of the performance spaces, the estimated audience attendance, and what theatre-goers can be expected to pay for the performance. Will you offer classes or workshops and will you charge for them? Again, information gathered from other arts groups in the community will be helpful even though you may be serving a very different audience and offering a very special type of theatre.

It may take some experimenting in the beginning to find what your market will bear. You may choose to have a price scale that varies with the type of audience you have. For instance, you may give a senior adult discount to individual audience members or you may have a flat performance-fee rate that will differentiate between a particular audience of low-income status and another audience attending a conference.

Earned income can be supplemented by concession sales of soft drinks, snacks, and items such as T-shirts, mugs, cookbooks, note cards, etc. This may involve more work than you want to handle, but in some cases, depending upon the audience, this may be a surprisingly lucrative source of revenue. Arts funding agencies like to see theatres earning as much as possible and often reward the efforts and ingenuity of a group making the most of its own resources.

Government Support
Governments can be a source of funding for nonprofit theatres. The federal government at this writing still supports the arts through the National Endowment for the Arts. Although there may be NEA projects for which senior adult theatres could qualify and you should acquaint yourself with their guidelines, much of this funding is distributed to states, and then small theatres can apply for money from state arts councils.

State legislatures, county commissions, and city councils sometimes appropriate money specifically for the arts or for arts projects. You may be able to go directly to these sources for funding, especially on a local level, or there may be arts councils set up for the specific purpose of distributing these funds.

You will be expected to follow specific formats to apply for and receive grants from these sources—forms to be completed by certain dates during the year, possibly followed by an in-person presentation of your project, and specific dates when grants are awarded. There are certain limitations on who may apply for funding from these agencies. Start with your local or state arts councils and local government administrative offices for information on these sources of arts funding. Many of these agencies have Web sites, and these are good places to begin your research.

There may be other money available through state and local governments to support projects especially for senior adults. For information on this resource, check with your local area agency on aging or your state commission on aging. Federal money from Title III funds from the Older Americans Act is distributed by states to county levels and to local agencies on aging for community-based services to the elderly. You may be able to interest your local agency in adopting your project and contributing to its funding, since it will serve senior adults within its area. The Seasoned Performers originated in and is still partly supported by such an agency.

Arts Funding Agencies
Special arts funding agencies or councils may be set up in your area to allow for efficient and fair allocations of community support. These agencies may be raising funds from various sources such as businesses, individuals, and perhaps government sources to form a pool of money for which

25

local arts groups may apply. Check your local or state arts councils or local chambers of commerce for information.

Both government and other funding agencies come with various regulations and rules. Much planning, record keeping, documentation, public recognition, and reporting will be required. However, the level of support may be enough to warrant the trouble, and the regulations demand that your project be run in a responsible manner.

These government and area arts agencies are charged with distributing money in an equitable way to serve populations in specific areas with a variety of good arts projects. In general they want to support artists with opportunities to do their work, to attract new artists and develop new audiences, to serve rural, inner-city, and/or suburban areas, and to include special populations. They are interested in outreach, education, partnerships, and exploring new art forms as well as in preserving traditional forms. Find out what priorities your agencies have. These are stated in the grant guidelines or can be given to you by a grants officer. If you can design projects that will dovetail with their particular objectives, you may have a better chance of receiving funding. Senior adult theatres by definition serve a special population, and this can be a distinct advantage in fund-raising.

However, the granting process can be very competitive. These agencies are looking at the quality of arts projects, the artists' credentials, and the track record of groups requesting funding. Make sure you are fully acquainted with the formats, criteria, and limitations of each individual agency before you begin planning a grant proposal. Make direct contact with an official before you proceed.

Foundations and Trusts

Grantmaking foundations and trusts of all sizes are established by companies, communities, and individuals or families to support charitable organizations and causes. These foundations and trusts are very specific in their goals and scope and give their funds to specific fields of interest, such as the arts, education, youth, etc. Many are very restrictive in focus; others give to a broad range of causes. Some give to organizations that serve small geographic areas; others give to projects that serve larger areas.

The Foundation Directory, published by the Foundation Center and found in most libraries, is an annual reference source for information about large foundations. It contains an alphabetical listing by state of the larger foundations and includes addresses, contact persons, areas of giving, types of grants, limitations, and application information. Other sources include *The Foundation Directory Part 2*, for smaller foundations, and the *National Directory of Corporate Giving*.

States also produce directories that list foundations and trusts in the state, with specific information that will be helpful to grant seekers. Perhaps this would be the best type of resource for small arts groups. Check your local library for a directory of this sort.

Communicate directly with an official of a foundation or trust before you try to apply so that you won't waste your time and effort on something that is not a possibility. A telephone call or a letter of inquiry will usually result in a quick answer. These officials are normally very helpful in supplying any information and assistance that you may need. Out of the vast quantity of these foundations and trusts, you will probably only locate a few to which your theatre project could apply. Look especially for those that give priority to arts organizations *and* the elderly and those that give aid to the same geographical area that you are serving.

Applying for Grants

To apply for any of the aforementioned grants, you will need to supply some very specific information by an established date. Make sure that you have all the information, guidelines, and forms necessary to apply for funding.

Usually, applicants are asked to supply certain information about their organization and documentation of IRS recognition as a 501(c)(3) organization. You may be asked to supply a narrative of your specific project, resumes of the administrative and artistic staff involved with the project, an itemized budget including expenses and income projections, and sources with documentation. Be expected to explain how your project will meet specific criteria for selection. This may include a detailed explanation of how your goals dovetail with the goals of the agency, evidence of your ability to implement the project and achieve quality, and evidence of the benefits and impact on the community.

Remember to emphasize the unique contributions to the arts and the community that your senior adult theatre can offer and the unique resources that you have. You are making theatre accessible to a constituency of older artists and audiences, possibly some with disabilities and limitations. These older artists have a rich heritage and a specific perspective on issues that can be showcased and celebrated. This can bring educational enrichment to audiences of all ages. You may have access to specific groups in the community who may not ordinarily attend arts events such as those in health-care or retirement facilities and senior centers. You may be bringing support to the arts from unusual sources such as area agencies on aging and groups of older populations. These aspects of senior adult theatre can add weight to your proposal when you are competing for arts funding. (See Appendix III for an example of a narrative of a grant proposal and response to evaluation criteria.)

Unless you are applying for "seed money" to start your theatre, you may also be asked to supply detailed financial and production history, certain statistics for earlier years such as number of productions, a breakdown of types of audiences reached, and other supporting materials. Therefore, it is important to keep these records as you develop your program. You may also be asked to supply a copy of a recent audit. Your proposal will need signatures of the officer(s) in charge of overseeing the project.

Even a successful proposal may receive only a portion of the requested funding. Therefore, it may be a good plan to seek the ultimate for your project but also plan how to proceed if you get less money than you solicit. Cushion your budget proposal with areas where you can cut back if necessary and still achieve your main goals. Talk to officials and look at listings of allocations for similar projects to get a feel for what range you might realistically expect—and then ask for a bit more.

Private Sector Funding

Private sector donations are an important source of funding for many arts groups and include both corporate and individual giving. Many large corporations regularly give part of their profits to charitable causes. Some may do this through their own foundation and have a process in place for such requests. Others may give large sums directly to an arts council for distribution, and some may be open to individual requests directly from arts groups. You can pinpoint corporations that give to the arts by checking with your local arts council, chamber of commerce, other arts groups, and newspapers or other publications. Contributors are often listed in programs of other arts groups' shows and concerts, and these lists can be a starting point.

It is helpful to remember that businesses are often motivated in their charitable giving at least partly by the public relations it offers them. Therefore, for a senior adult theatre, look for businesses that have large numbers of senior adult clients. These may be large utilities, banks, drug companies, investment companies, production companies that make products used by older adults, etc. Offer some public recognition for donations, as listings in programs or announcements at performances. Perhaps you can display names of supporters in some of your publicity materials.

Personal contacts do help in all forms of fund-raising. Make use of the contacts of your senior adult participants. Where did they work? Of what groups are they members? Compile a list of contacts' names, addresses, and telephone numbers. Perhaps you can ask your participants to make initial contacts to pave the way for a more formal inquiry about donations.

For businesses that do not have a specified format for applying for donations, prepare an information packet including statistics on the outreach potential of your troupe, what you can offer as public relations, good photographs along with a history of your program and description of the project, and a request for funding. Try to speak in person to an official from a business that is a potential donor. For large corporations, there will be a special officer who handles charitable giving. For small businesses, try to contact the owner, president, or a vice president.

Individual donations may tend to be smaller for a senior adult theatre because these theatres may be less widely seen by the public and may be less socially prominent and because many of the supporters may be on fixed incomes. However, this resource can be significant and should not be overlooked in an annual fund drive. Start by building a mailing list from your audiences; family and friends of participants; and lists of patrons from other arts groups, arts councils, and other clubs and organizations. This mailing list can be utilized in marketing as well as in seeking donations. Keep the list small enough to be manageable for direct mailings, which will contain information, special offers, and requests for donations *and* for follow-up mailings of reminders and updates. Be prepared to reward your donors in some way, with listings in programs, priority tickets, or special events.

One of the *least* effective attempts to raise funds by The Seasoned Performers was a direct mailer request for donations once sent to seven hundred individuals in the community. In retrospect, there were a number of reasons for the small return on this particular effort: (1) the mailing list used was too large for a follow-up of any sort, (2) the list used was of residents in certain geographic areas and was unspecified in terms of interests and activities of individuals, (3) there was no public event or publicity connected with the request other than our usual rather "closed-circuit" tour, and (4) there were no additional benefits offered to donors other than contributing to the "good cause" of the senior adult theatre. More people responded by asking about joining or scheduling performances than by making donations.

Fund-Raisers

Special fund-raisers may be included in annual campaigns for funding or can be utilized for capital campaigns for funding particular needs of the program. If the senior adult participants of a theatre are involved in a special fund-raising project, it is important to consider their energy limits as well as their unique potential. The production requirements of the theatre may be enough for the actors and crew, and it may be too much to ask them to also participate in some outside project that would put a strain on their energy and time. There are ways in which senior adults can be especially gifted in raising funds; however, it

31

may be hoped that your board or "friends" of the theatre handle the organization for these events.

Special performances; parties; wine-tastings; raffle sales; garage sales; crafts, cookbook, or bake sales; auctions; even bowling or rock-a-thons can be fun as well as effective fund-raisers. To be successful, these projects need extensive and realistic planning and coordination, good timing, a sufficient number of people involved, and donated goods or services.

The most effective fund-raiser done by The Seasoned Performers was a cookbook/storybook that combined company members' recipes and memories. There were several crucial elements that made this effort succeed: (1) It was a good product. These people can cook *and* tell stories! (2) A percentage of the publishing cost was donated. This meant we could sell it at a reasonable price and realize a profit sooner. (3) We sold it on tour, where it was seen by dozens of different audiences. (4) The timing was good. We worked on it during an off time in the summer and sold it during the fall, when holiday presents were on everyone's mind. (5) The entire company contributed to the book and sold copies independently to family and friends. (6) A realistic number of books were printed. We sold out—raising fully one-third of the cost of a brand-new fifteen-passenger van.

Starting Small and Growing

Since it seems that a senior adult theatre benefits mainly a special segment of a community, it may be reasonable to expect the funding to be rather small in the beginning. As the community becomes more aware of the quality and real benefits of such a theatre, the support will also grow. But this can take time and tenacity. In the beginning, a small senior adult theatre may be required to do more in the way of special fund-raisers to generate enough money to cover a season. Gradually, more substantial grants may be added as the theatre becomes recognized as a solid entity producing worthwhile projects and as the personnel becomes more acquainted with the processes involved.

To ensure that a senior adult theatre does move toward its full potential in both programming and funding it is helpful to divide its long-range planning into three- to five-year increments aimed at achieving these goals. These plans should include creating budgets that grow by degrees and allow for specific aims to be reached. They should cover the development of new funding that will allow these budgets to be met. They should entail ways in which the theatre might become eligible for more funding—such as adding outreach and education—and for acquiring equipment or other large-expense items. These plans should be realistic in both the growth of programming and funding but should take the theatre closer to its ultimate goals.

There is an ongoing problem with many small arts groups besides the annual struggle for securing enough funding. This dilemma is that the planners can never predict with certainty exactly how much money will be generated during the year. How many audience members will actually come—and pay? What grants will actually be awarded and for how much? Will the fund-raiser be successful? How can we plan a season if we don't know how much money we will have? These questions can be especially hard to answer in the early years of a theatre.

The first solution in dealing with this problem is to secure one solid, ongoing source that you can count on from year to year. This might be the income from an endowment; support from a larger entity such as a university, an area agency on aging, or a senior adult organization; or a multiyear commitment from a corporation, foundation, or individual. As long as you know you can depend on a certain level of funding, you can proceed into your fiscal year with more confidence. You can begin programming based on this funding and plan for other goals contingent upon receiving applied-for grants or on completing an effective fund-raiser.

The second answer for this problem of uncertain funding is to build a "contingency" or "support" fund that would be separate from your annual operating budget. This could be an important asset for a healthy theatre, since there may well be lean years or periods of cash-flow problems. This emergency account can be built with special fund-raisers for that purpose or a large contribution by a donor or collected in small amounts over several years. The growth of this fund can be included in long-range plans. Once established, this fund can ensure that advance planning and work on projects can proceed in a timely manner so that the theatre is more able to meet its programming and artistic potential. The fund can also add to earned income with the interest that it can accrue.

. . .

As a theatre gets older and more established, it becomes easier to predict a year's income with a degree of accuracy because of past experience and knowledge of the sources and processes. Let your fund-raising efforts grow gradually as your personnel is able to handle the demands. Don't try to do everything at once in the beginning. It is better to try to balance your artistic efforts with select fund-raising efforts that you can handle with thoroughness. Over time you will learn what is most effective for your theatre and you can develop a broad enough base of funding for sufficient support.

3

Attracting and Accommodating Senior Adults

As in all theatres, the most valuable asset to a senior adult theatre is its people—performers, directors, technicians and crew members, and other active supporters. Although most theatres want to attract the most experienced, talented, and qualified personnel possible, many senior adult theatres have a rather inclusive philosophy and want to offer opportunities for older individuals who want to explore and learn.

In a theatre that is especially for seniors, many of these participants may be fifty-five years of age and well above. The Seasoned Performers troupe ranges in age from around fifty to eighty-seven, with the majority of members in their sixties and seventies. This chapter suggests ways of attracting and recruiting participants, making accommodations for older adults, and keeping volunteers.

Motivation

Why does anyone choose to work with a senior adult theatre? Recognizing and understanding some of the possible motivations and needs of the participants can help a theatre program set goals and design the processes to achieve these goals.

Many older people have simply loved working in theatre or going to theatre for most of their lives and want to continue to be active in this rewarding art. They are looking for a theatre home where they can practice their craft in a modified arena. Some have had little or no experience but have always wanted to try this activity and, in retirement, finally have the time. Others just want to learn something new and want to challenge and stimulate their minds and imaginations. Theatre is fun, creative, and interactive and can offer different and exciting ways of developing and expressing oneself.

But there are other, perhaps less obvious reasons for wanting to work with a senior adult theatre. Sometimes the changes in life that come with retirement, diminished physical abilities, loss of spouses and friends, and altered lifestyles can create reduced social interaction, a loss of other activities, and a feeling of lost identity.

Some people have enjoyed an active place in the community, in the workplace, or in their families that has changed drastically at a later stage in life. One of The Seasoned Performers says, "Although I held a position for a number of years that had provided a degree of recognition in the community and in a professional group, I suddenly discovered when I retired I was just another 'senior citizen.' I needed much more than a social outlet. I needed to be part of a group that was making a contribution."

Working in a theatre designed for senior adults can lead to a new role in life—a new identity—and a validation of one's productivity and abilities. Theatre can give participants a new way to use the experiences and memories collected over many years. Not only is there social interaction and support from a group of individuals actively working and learning together, but participants can continue to feel needed and appreciated for their unique gifts to the community.

Attracting Older Participants

Although there may be truth in the lines "If you build it, they will come," you may also discover that some older adults resist actively committing to participate in a senior adult theatre. Veteran actors may be concerned about the quality of such a theatre or may resist the image of the term *senior adult*. People with no experience in theatre may fear the idea of performing or memorizing, may be uncertain of their physical adequacy, or may resist a large and continuing time commitment.

Not only will you want to attract participants as you start your theatre, but with each new season it is important to consider how to add new associates. Because of the realities of higher probabilities of health crises and diminishing abilities of older actors—and their spouses—recruitment is a priority in maintaining a senior adult theatre.

Understanding the needs of the age group that you are targeting is the first step in designing a program to fill these needs. Learn as much as you can about this general population from books and articles on the subject, from professionals in the field of aging, and from association with older individuals. The resources in this field are many. You may start with the National Council on Aging, the Administration on Aging, or the American Association of Retired Persons (AARP), all of which have Web sites that can lead you to information. You could check a local college or university department of gerontology, a local area agency on aging, or the social sciences area of a library for books and more information.

It is recommended that you not only have a knowledge of the effects of aging and the concerns of this general population but also that you understand specific groups that your theatre may serve both as participants and audiences.

37

You may expect to work with a group of people such as those connected with a retirement community or senior center, a number of theatre veterans who wish to be a part of your theatre, or a much broader group living in your geographic area. Try to **involve individuals in the planning** so that they will feel part of the theatre program from the beginning. Find out what they want. In what kinds of activities would they like to participate? What might attract them and what might deter them from participating? Discovering their ideas, expectations, concerns, and desires can help you in planning engaging, nonthreatening activities and in choosing appropriate material—and you will have an easier job of recruiting others.

The **professional competence of your personnel** can be one of the most effective elements in attracting people. Abilities of the staff or leaders are important not only in the area of theatre they have experience in but also in the caring, understanding, and motivating personalities they possess. Prospective members look not only at the theatrical results but at the way the older actors are treated. It may take a unique kind of theatre professional to work successfully with older adults. Choose these leaders carefully.

Once you have an established organization, the most attractive element is a group of **enthusiastic and interesting people doing creative work**. A newer member of The Seasoned Performers says, "Everyone looked like they were having so much fun, I wanted to join them!" Keeping members active and happy is one of your ongoing considerations for recruitment as well as for programming.

One the most effective means of attracting participants is **word of mouth**. Friends and acquaintances of actively interested persons are far more likely to feel comfortable coming around with someone for the first time. Encourage company members to invite people they know and meet to participate. This is a good way to tap into unknown talent. By this same token, personal invitations from you to those that you may especially want to attract can be very effective.

A **welcoming invitation to an organizational or "open meeting"** can be less daunting than an announcement of auditions, although of course you may want to hold auditions for a particular production. Announcements for such open meetings and auditions should clearly state that senior adults are especially welcome and that no experience is necessary.

Offering a **variety of ways to participate in the theatre** is encouraging for those who would like to get their feet wet only a little at first. These ways may include production and support committees, workshops and classes, and a reading performance group as well as roles in a play. This information, given at an open meeting, along with overall organizational makeup and objectives, future plans, and specific time requirements, will help make people more comfortable with signing up to work or in deciding to audition. Have something specific planned that can bring them back soon for another activity. Try to give a specific date and activity to anyone who calls to inquire about participating. If you don't **get them active with something right away**, you may risk losing a recruit.

Be sure to communicate the **potential contribution** that the theatre can make to your audiences. It is a particularly compelling notion that participants can have fun, develop and use their skills, and give pleasure, inspiration, and ideas to others.

If your theatre is open to seniors in the community, **getting the word out to this special constituency** can be done effectively in a variety of ways (see Chapter Six on marketing for more details):

- Create a press release and a flyer announcing an open meeting or an audition. This should include information such as identity of the group; sponsoring organizations; the purpose of the meeting; the date, time, and place of the meeting; and who is invited. Include contact name and telephone number for more information.
- Use all the usual media outlets such as arts sections of newspapers, local television and radio public service announcements and talk shows, and flyers posted in public places. Also send your press releases to any special sections of the newspaper that aim their appeal to older adults as well as to special publications for senior citizens. Try to interest local newspapers in doing a feature article—on personalities, success stories, the new group in town, etc.—that will be published before an open meeting. Feature articles with photographs can be a very effective means of recruitment.
- Send your flyers to church senior adult ministries, library groups, retirement facilities where residents are active, senior centers, literary clubs, theatres, and area agencies on aging. (This same listing will be used for marketing your shows and workshops.)
- Make a presentation in person at meetings at these sites. This can be effective for recruiting members as well as for bookings. Taking several participants with you to do a short performance and "make a pitch" can produce far more results than sending a flyer for the leader to read or post. These efforts take time, however, and may be restricted to your initial organization or perhaps tried periodically when you especially need new participants or have a show to promote. You might want to commit to doing one of these presentations each month or another workable schedule.
- Keep your brochure visible. Public buildings and

offices may have brochure display stands. There may be display opportunities available at senior adult conferences and special events. You might try to get the brochure included in newcomers packets provided by banks or the chamber of commerce. Consider enclosing a brochure in mailings.

- Send your own theatre newsletter to a list of prospective members and interested parties. This is an excellent way to keep your constituents informed of your activities and can attract new participants.
- Include an invitation to join or audition in any programs printed for your productions.

Offering a short-term activity in which older participants can test the waters, learn new skills, and get to know each other can be very helpful in establishing a group that may then be willing to audition or commit to a more long-term project. These activities could include a workshop in acting, improvisation, or Creative Dramatics. It could be a production of a ten-minute play, a short series of monologues, or a reading program that can be done rather quickly and presented for a small audience.

Auditions for a senior theatre production should be as reassuring and as egalitarian as possible. This process can be stressful, and older performers will often take it very seriously. Try to create a relaxed atmosphere and make sure that those who do not get a role have the option of participating in another way, such as serving on a production committee or working on another project. If you have auditionees read from a prepared script, try to have large, bold-print scripts available. Also allow time for second readings for those not satisfied with their first attempts. Remember that it may take a personal invitation to convince an older person to audition.

41

When you are auditioning individuals whom you do not know well, use several activities other than simply reading from the script, such as theatre games, improvising in groups, following specific physical directions, etc. Working in these ways can help relax the auditionees, and it can also help you spot abilities and problems. If a time arises when you have to make a difficult decision about an individual, let your priorities guide you. Protecting the quality of the experience for all the participants, the good of the theatre, and the good of the show may help you avoid unhappy situations.

Training New Thespians

In responding to the needs of older adults who would like to participate but who are lacking specific theatre experience, a senior adult theatre can serve as a training base. This may be in the form of small roles in a play, understudy roles, positions as support personnel who will be able to observe the rehearsal and production processes, or in the way of classes or workshops.

In your play selection process, consider the roles available for inexperienced actors as well as the challenge and attractiveness of roles for veteran actors. If all of your actors are likely to be very inexperienced, you can start with very short plays requiring a limited amount of memorization.

Periodic workshops in acting, improvisation, technical theatre, etc. led by a theatre professional can be very attractive activities for senior adults looking for new experiences and may be the launching pad for further work in theatre. *The Golden Stage: Dramatic Activities for Older Adults* (McDonough 1994) and its accompanying *The Golden Stage: Dramatic Activities for Older Adults*

Teacher's Guide, second edition (McDonough 1998), are good resources for a workshop of this sort. Used in combination, these books give specific lessons and activities for a drama workshop especially for older students. The teacher's guide contains a section on understanding the older student and an extensive bibliography—including books on aging as well as the theatre—which can be an extremely helpful resource in preparing to work with older adults in a theatre program.

Special Considerations and Accommodations

You may be working with people in a very broad age range who are experiencing wide variances in the effects of aging. In general, an older population will begin to experience a slowing of responses and diminished sensory perceptions, energy and strength, and flexibility. Some may be coping with chronic physical problems, loneliness, fear, or depression as well. A senior adult theatre should give special attention to understanding and accommodating the needs of this population.

What exactly can you expect of mature actors and crew members? Can they memorize lines, follow directions, remember cues and blocking? The answer is usually a resounding *yes!* It may take seniors a longer period of time and more repetition to memorize and feel confident in the pattern of action for a play, but, in general, most healthy seniors will be able to memorize. Illness, medications, and aging can, however, take their toll on anyone's powers of concentration. And there may be those who simply don't want to commit to the work necessary to memorize lines. For those who have a real problem with memorizing, it is best to offer another way to participate—nonspeaking roles, improvisations, a readers theatre group, support committees, or classes. If you are creating a theatre for a group of residents or others with memory or concentration loss, your overall programming should be geared toward their abilities.

An entire chapter of this book is devoted to space considerations in planning a senior adult theatre program. Special thought must be given to accessibility, safety, surrounding environment, and comfort. See Chapter Five for more details on space and technical considerations. Chapter Four focuses on programming and material possibilities for a senior adult theatre. The following section contains a collection of suggestions, based on experience with The Seasoned Performers, which can generally make the work easier, safer, more comfortable, and more effective or efficient with older participants:

- Leaders should communicate very clearly the goals, the processes and procedures, and the ground rules.
- Use as many printed instructions as you can to minimize misunderstanding due to hearing problems. Practice your best stage projection and diction when speaking to a group.
- Scripts and all written material should be available in slightly enlarged type with a high degree of contrast, perhaps double-spaced.
- Try to schedule your activities during the daytime or early evening and during times of the year when extreme weather conditions are less likely to make any necessary travel hazardous.
- Individual sessions of classes or rehearsals should be held to a maximum of about two hours with a break after one hour—or sooner if it seems advisable. Avoid requiring long periods of sitting or standing.
- Rehearsal and production work should extend over a

longer period of time, such as six to eight weeks instead of four to six. Avoid rehearsing every day of the week for most of this time.

- Rehearsal schedules should include immediate review sessions of sections of blocking, etc. to help reinforce short-term memory. It is usually helpful to work with no more than about ten pages of script at a rehearsal session and to review those ten pages at the succeeding rehearsal.

- It may be necessary to schedule special line rehearsals for the cast or offer individual help for those who have more trouble with memorizing.

- Expect to have to adapt blocking or action requirements occasionally to accommodate an actor's specific disability. You may have to cut, simplify, or change a bit of action to make it workable for an actor.

- It may sometimes be necessary to repeat directions. Verbal repetition of instructions not only helps with memory but can make the words clearer for older ears.

- It is a helpful policy to require the actors and crew to *write down* "notes" given after rehearsal. Providing them with a notebook and pencil can encourage this habit. Give them adequate time to write these notes and to write clear blocking directions in their scripts.

- It is desirable, when feasible, to use an understudy system or double cast the show. Over the period of a rehearsal and run of a show, health and other crises can crop up and threaten to ruin a production. If the time commitment for a production is especially long, this system can also allow the participants the freedom to travel. This kind of flexibility in scheduling can be important to those who like to visit grandchildren or take advantage of the many travel opportunities available to older adults.

- It is a good idea to use personal contact and telephone calls to remind participants of events when there is a lapse of time—a week or more—between the original announcement and the occurrence. A printed handout in the form of a calendar is helpful but may be overlooked as life's many distractions take place. A telephone call is often a bit of interaction that is meaningful in establishing social ties and may help motivate a participant on a more personal level.
- If possible, equip telephones that will be used at rehearsal or in the office with volume control on the handsets to accommodate those users with slight hearing loss.
- Adequate seating should be provided in rooms that are used for class or rehearsal. If you are using metal folding chairs, you can make them more comfortable by tying on inexpensive foam cushions.
- The volume and quality of an individual's voice can be affected by age factors. You may need to rely on an amplification system to assure the sound quality of your shows, especially if the space is large. Use of a body microphone on each actor is best, if purchase or rental is feasible in your budget.
- Don't ask a senior adult cast or crew to lift heavy scenery or equipment, to climb on ladders, or to use dangerous tools.
- Older eyes cannot adjust quickly to darkness. If you are using normal stage lighting, avoid going to full blackouts. Give a "glow" for actors to get on and off stage. Backstage will need more "stumble" lights. Avoid total darkness.
- Keep a file handy with emergency numbers and personal information on each company member including address and home telephone, special health considerations, whom to inform in case of an emergency and

how to reach these individuals, the name and telephone numbers of the primary care physician and any other doctors who should be notified, and hospital preference.

While it is necessary to make special accommodations for older participants, it is best not to constantly dwell on age. No one needs or wants to be constantly reminded of getting older. Make the adjustments as a matter of course and get on with creative endeavors.

Keeping Participants in the Theatre

It is essential to the theatre company's survival that members of the troupe want to work on project after project and stay active in the theatre over a period of time. This not only assures that there is a core of workers who are learning and gaining from experience, forming a company that works well together, and thus raising the quality of the theatre's efforts, but it can help add new members who are attracted by the people involved.

Everyone, at any age, wants to be treated with respect and valued for his or her efforts and achievements. In senior adult theatre this is especially important to remember, since many of the participants may be dealing with changing self-images and loss of identity and confidence. Leaders will have far more success in keeping members of the troupe and in achieving worthwhile results if they possess a true appreciation of older adults, a sense of humor, and a positive, encouraging attitude. This is true whether the leaders are older or younger than most of the participants.

It is important to expect good work and professional attitudes from the older company and to avoid condescending, impersonal, or dishonest treatment. The leaders should also be very confident in their own knowledge and skills of theatre. A certain strength of leadership is often necessary. Mutual respect is a key element in a successful senior adult theatre.

You will usually find that senior adults want to do good work. They will be able to recognize a stageworthy achievement, but they are also dependent, as are virtually all who work in theatre, on the responses of others. The response of the director or leader is as important as the response of the audience. Being honestly complimentary of the efforts of members of the company and being sensitive to their feelings can impart confidence that will improve the quality of performances as well as encourage individuals to stick around to work on another show.

Besides providing **opportunities for active participation and growth in creative and challenging artistic endeavors**, remember the **goals of social interaction and gaining a new sense of identity**. These elements of the experience can be enhanced by attention to experiences other than the actual theatre processes.

Veteran actors of all ages talk about the camaraderie involved in working in the theatre. To further the opportunities for bonding, theatre people have always found ways to relax, socialize, and celebrate together. The "cast party" may be considered by some to be one of the best rewards of all the hard work involved. This idea of providing more **social occasions** is important for senior adults but may need a bit of adapting to the circumstances.

It may be too physically demanding to hold such an event immediately following a performance unless it is a very limited affair. Perhaps some simple refreshments provided by people who are not involved in the show will suffice for this moment. This reception may include the audience and will give the company an important chance to receive compliments.

At a later time, the company may feel more prepared for a larger event. It may be better for these get-togethers to happen in the daytime. A simple Dutch treat lunch can provide a relaxed opportunity for conversation. Another popular idea is to arrange a showing of a videotape of the show.

A worthwhile item to try to include in your theatre's budget is an annual "appreciation" or "celebration" luncheon or reception for everyone who has worked in the theatre during the year. This can give participants something to anticipate and offers a tangible reward for their efforts. It can also help establish identity with the group. A celebration does not have to be expensive to be effective in raising the morale of all involved. If your budget won't allow it, the participants can share the cost. Look for opportunities for other social events at regular intervals throughout the year.

Memorabilia can be especially meaningful and fun for senior adults. T-shirts, caps, mugs, tote bags, and personalized business cards can help publicize a show and the theatre and can give the company member a sense of belonging. It is well worth the expense if you can find the budget for any of these items. Some of these could also be sold to audiences for revenue.

Photographing and videotaping the show will be valuable not only in chronicling the work of your theatre and in publicizing its events but in providing a tangible memory for your company. Members can order reprints to show to family and friends and perhaps begin a scrapbook of their new adventure. Always arrange for photographs to be taken at a special session. Flashbulbs during a show can be distracting and actually disabling to some eyes. Remember that taping requires the author's consent even if you have rights to perform the play.

Personal touches can be significant to senior adults. The theatre may well become an important source of emotional support for its members. Small expressions of concern such as a personal telephone call or a card can mean a lot to an individual. It is a good idea to keep a supply of sympathy, get well, special thank-you, and cheering cards to send individuals at different times of need. Encourage members to keep in touch with one another and let the theatre know about the welfare of its "family."

Finally, it is important that the theatre not wear out its participants. Schedule your activities to give them **time for rest and recuperation**. Give your company time to do other things. Avoid overscheduling holiday times of the year, when there are many other activities going on. Balance this idea with the planning of regular events so that participants don't drift away due to lack of action!

Special Audiences

Although you may not target only senior adults as audience members, it certainly makes sense that you may want to make a special effort to attract them and accommodate their interests and needs. Making live theatre accessible for disabled audience members may be a primary goal. More is discussed on these audiences in the chapters on space and technical considerations, programming and material, and marketing. It is worth mentioning here that the same thought processes are valuable for serving older audiences as in accommodating participants. Understanding their motivations in terms of interests, needs, and physical limitations will lead to similarly unique accommodations.

There will be a wide variety in older audiences. Those confined to a facility may want mainly musical revues, light comedies, or stories, whereas yet-active audiences may accept more thought-provoking dramas addressing issues with which they are still concerned.

One of the many letters of appreciation from audience members was especially meaningful to The Seasoned Performers. It read, ". . . I stay depressed and bewildered most of the time. I had decided I was feeling too low to go and hear people laugh. I just want to say to you that I . . . came away feeling so light-hearted and it meant so much to me. . . . Thank you for helping me feel better."

Another individual spoke for many audience members when she said, "It's so rare for me to identify with every character in a play . . . and these actors inspired me!" The vigor and courage of older actors can inspire all ages. A fifth grader wrote, "When I become a grandmother I would really like to become a part of the Season[ed] Performers."

. . .

Senior adult theatre is special. Attention must be paid to the needs of the participants as well as to any specific audiences you may be targeting. The more you learn about, listen to, and work with these special populations, the more successful you will be at devising creative ways to make it possible for them to take part in the joys of theatre *and* the more successful your theatre will be at maintaining a core group of enthusiastic participants.

4

Programming and Performance Material

Like community theatre in general, senior adult theatres encompass a broad scope of programming and performance material. Their descriptions range from the fullest programming of training, performances, touring, and even professional opportunities to the simplest profiles of informal theatre fun. Some programs include a variety of productions played for a broad general audience, others play mainly for residents and friends, and yet others may involve participation in theatre activities for personal satisfaction and never result in a performance at all. Some programs are created to serve older participants and audiences only; others span generations in both areas.

Performance material ranges from simple readings, oral histories, short plays, or musical revues to more fully developed plays with more complex plots and themes. Material may be created within the troupe, found in play catalogs or anthologies of plays specifically for older adults, or commissioned from a writer.

A consideration in selecting material is the ability to obtain the rights to use it. Check the current copyright laws before you begin choosing material for use by your theatre. The laws apply to all venues, regardless of whether you are charging admission for a performance. Your local library can give you information on these copyright laws. Catalogs containing play listings have information about obtaining rights and whether there will be a royalty. If royalty payments are prohibitive, you can inquire about a waiver, choose a royalty-free script or material in the public domain—that published before a certain date or which is not copyrighted—or create your own material.

Many factors will guide you in planning for specific programming, such as your mission; the desires of all involved; the makeup of the company and the other constituents you are serving; resources such as time, space, and funding; availability of theatre professionals; and so on. Your programming may develop as your resources develop over time. Consider the options and choose the elements that suit your circumstances and needs.

Do you want to produce a traditional "season" of plays with a certain number and variety of productions planned for the year? Will you do musical revues, readers theatre, short dramas? Will you develop oral histories or improvisations with your participants? Will you offer classes or workshops? Will you concentrate on theatre activities with no performance attached? Will you tour? Will you be working strictly with older participants, or will there be opportunities for intergenerational activities? Will you serve a largely senior adult audience, or will you include a variety of ages?

While there is no single description of a senior adult theatre, many such theatres around the country have taken a realistic look at their options and have successfully launched a unique type of programming to suit their particular needs, desires, and resources. The following examples represent the broad scope of possibilities in programming and material. (See Appendix II for contact information.)

The Range of Existing Programs

Since 1978, Stagebridge, in Oakland, California, has been developing its broad range of programming. It now offers a theatre-training program for seniors; a public performance season; a community tour for clubs, senior facilities, and organizations; a storytelling program for schools; and an intergenerational literacy program. Its public performances include productions especially written for Stagebridge as well as theatre "classics." The company's name defines its main goal—"to bridge the generation gap through the wonders of theatre."

The Slightly Older Adult Players (SOAP), in Colorado, places its emphasis on two major shows: a holiday theme show featuring music, skits, poetry, etc. given in early December and a full-length play, often a melodrama, presented at its host senior center in late spring. The plays are chosen from a catalog such as Samuel French or Dramatists Play Service or written by a member of the company. The troupe of about thirty players also participates in theatre-related activities just for enjoyment, such as play reading, charades, improvisational work, impromptu skits, etc. This enthusiastic company boasts two spin-off groups who also perform: a musical arm called SOAP Tones and a dance troupe called SOAP Toes, who entertain on tour in the community and the senior center.

Footsteps of the Elders, in Ohio, is a small ensemble company made up of women that presents minimalist productions emphasizing the events of women's lives, all based on the members' reminiscences. They have worked with improvisations, commissioned a play, and collaborated with teenagers and others creating plays based on memories. This company tours locally, nationally, and internationally.

The Merry Clements Players is a troupe of actors and actresses, all over fifty years of age, who tour nursing homes, retirement centers, and senior recreation centers in Colorado with comedies and skits, some of which have been written by members of the group. Other material is selected from short pieces written especially for senior adults. Some of their productions are geared for elementary and middle schools, where they also tour. This troupe stresses fun above all, not only in the plays but in preparing for the performances. Casting is done so that everyone who wants to perform can have a role.

Kirkwood Accomplished Thespian Society, in a retirement community in Alabama, uses all royalty-free material, sometimes drawing from plays written for young people found in the youth sections of the library, sometimes dramatizing folktales or reading other stories. No attention is placed on the age of the characters, as these thespians read aloud for pleasure and occasionally do a production for their fellow residents. Costumes and props for these productions are found or provided by the participants. They have toured on occasion to another venue such as a library or church.

Curtain Time Retirement Vignettes, in Michigan, is a new improvisation senior theatre that presents skits and plays without scripts. Using its vignettes to increase its audiences' awareness of the challenges and opportunities in career planning and family adaptations in the years after fifty, this group plays for companies, clubs, marriage-enhancement groups, and other venues.

Sometimes the unique skills of the leaders or members of the troupe will define the type of programming and material for a theatre. The director of the Ripe and Ready Players in Tennessee developed a show consisting of a series of vignettes based on conversations with older adults focusing on their issues of interest. These conversations sparked the ideas for the show's dialogue and songs written by the director, who also serves as accompanist for the troupe. This group performs at schools and retirement and community centers as well as at Equity theatres and has played at the Spoleto Festival in Charleston, South Carolina.

The Seasoned Performers' programming includes touring with its newly commissioned plays and its repertory of reading programs to audiences of all ages and workshops focused on developing new skills. Material for performances has come from improvisations, poetry, and stories as well as the commissioned scripts. The plays have been lighthearted comedies with some underlying educational value designed to appeal to older audiences and to young students. Future possibilities include producing oral histories and some of the more recently available scripts for senior adults for matinee performances at a community theatre.

Short Plays and Monologues Especially for Seniors

The play's the thing—for many theatres—and locating and choosing one for a senior adult theatre has been a sticking point in the past. Physical and technical requirements, subject matter, and the roles in many available plays do not always fit the capabilities or interests of a senior adult theatre. As more theatres of this type have been created, however, short plays have been written especially for senior adults. These plays offer relevant and up-to-date subject matter, older roles, more roles for women, simple technical requirements, and a minimum of memorization. The very short variety can be produced in a flexible format of several plays, perhaps including monologues to complete a full program.

Resources for short plays for older adults include catalogs such as Dramatic Publishing Company, I. E. Clark Publications, and Bakers Plays. Several anthologies contain a number of plays for older adults: *New Plays for Mature Actors*, edited by Bonnie L. Vorenberg (1987, Coach House Press, available through Dramatic Publishing); and *Short Stuff: Ten- to Twenty-Minute Plays for Mature Actors*, compiled and edited by Ann McDonough (1998, Dramatic Publishing). The latter volume contains very short plays and includes a brief history and review of this particular genre. McDonough's *New Monologues for Mature Actors* (1997, Dramatic Publishing) contains pieces for older actors that may be used for auditions but might also be used as part of an evening of monologues and short plays. This book also has helpful suggestions for working on the pieces and memorizing them and lists other sources of monologues that would be suitable for mature actors. Her book *A Grand Entrance: Scenes and Monologues for Mature Actors* (1999, Dramatic Publishing) adds yet more choices for her readers. *21 Humorous, New Short Plays and Skits for Performing Grandparents* (1998) by Robert O. Redd is a no-royalty script book. Winner of the 1998 Gold Medal Mature Media Award, the book can be ordered from Thornapple Publishing Company. *Seniors Acting Up: Humorous New One-Act Plays and Skits for Older Adults* (1996), edited by Ted W. Fuller, contains one-act plays and skits plus miscellany such as coping with stage fright, how to audition, and vocal exercises. It can be ordered from Pleasant Hill Press.

It will be helpful to familiarize yourself with these publishers and others through up-to-date copies of their catalogs. These sources will contain listings of the newest plays as they are published. See Appendix II for contact information.

Appendix I of this book contains a list and description of one-act plays commissioned and produced by The Seasoned Performers and available from the playwrights. Information on other plays written for older actors is available through the Senior Adult Theatre Program at the University of Nevada–Las Vegas, Department of Theatre Arts.

Creating Performance Material Within the Group

In order to provide a role for everyone in the group or to suit the unique qualities and abilities of the troupe, a senior adult theatre may choose to produce theatrical material that has been created within the group. Under the guidance of a skilled leader, workshops aimed at introducing participants to acting, improvisation, or other aspects of drama and performing are valuable for developing skills, knowledge, and confidence. Some workshops can lead to a performance piece.

The Golden Stage: Dramatic Activities for Older Adults (1994) by Ann McDonough and its accompanying *The Golden Stage: Teacher's Guide* (1998), available through Dramatic Publishing Company, offer practical suggestions for creating musical and oral history revues as well as introducing senior adults to acting. The books also contain listings of other plays appropriate for senior adult theatre. *Acting Up!* (1982), by Marcie Telander, Flora Quinlan, and Karol Verson (Coach House Press, available through Dramatic Publishing) records the experiences of a touring improvisational troupe and offers techniques and exercises aimed at using life experiences to create oral histories and other performance material. *Making It Up As You Go Along* by Suzanne Carter (available through the author) uses the author's experience with the Ripe and Ready Players in Chattanooga, Tennessee, to describe the process of collecting material through interviews with older people and using this to create scenes and songs for a production. The book also contains additional information on working in senior adult theatre.

Commissioning Scripts

Having a script tailor-made for your theatre can ensure that you have a script that fits the group's interests and goals, has roles suited to specific actors, has reasonable production requirements, and gives unlimited rights to perform the work. The Seasoned Performers evolved into this process early on in its development to solve the problem of finding appropriate scripts and to tap into funding available for commissioning and producing scripts by local writers. Commissioning scripts continues to be a major focus for this theatre. The following suggestions come from The Seasoned Performers' fifteen years of experience in this process.

Finding a Writer

The most obvious starting point in the process of finding a suitable writer to create a script especially for your group may be to look for writers who have already written successful scripts for senior adults or for other types of theatres. Check any of the anthologies of plays for senior adults. You might inquire of other theatres that commission scripts. Children's theatres are a surprisingly rich source of creative, inventive writers who often can adapt their skills to suit senior adults.

You may wish to use a writer from your area who may be more aware of regional language and issues suited to your group. Look at nearby university theatre departments that offer playwriting courses. These professors may be interested in writing for a theatre group that will actually produce the work or may point you toward good students—all of whom aren't young anymore. Explore local and state writers' enclaves. Your local library can help you locate these.

Advertise your needs in a state or regional writers journal. Again, ask a librarian to assist you in finding such a publication, or check the Internet. Invite samples of a writer's work. Perhaps you will find not only a playwright but also a play.

The more you know about the writer's sensibilities, knowledge, humor, creativity, and ability to meet deadlines, the better. Try to see and/or read as much as you can of a writer's previous work. Check references just as you would when hiring a permanent employee. Work with the best writer that you can possibly afford and one who is willing and able to adapt his or her work to suit your needs.

Working with a Writer

Once you have chosen a writer, there are several specific items that should be agreed upon before contracts are signed. The writer should be presented with a complete list of any **special requirements or considerations** for the script. The following is an example of the topics of such a list:

1. audiences—ages, numbers, physical and other limitations, any special needs or interests, level of sophistication
2. actors—availability in terms of age, gender, physical limitations, acting experience or ability; desirable cast size
3. language—style, level of sophistication, and amount to memorize
4. technical considerations—playing spaces (does the play tour?), length of run, any limitations in settings

and set changes, numbers of scenes, sound, lighting, furniture, props, and costumes

5. subject matter—any specific topics of interest, desirable themes, or subjects to avoid

6. general—optimum length of play, type or style, any desired messages, limitations in the action required

A writer should be willing to work within the limitations and requirements. Often these points will actually help the creative process both by narrowing the focus and demanding imaginative thinking. Creative solutions to unique problems can result in theatrical jewels.

The **steps of production of script**, the **review process**, and a **time line** should be agreed upon and included in the contract with the writer. These steps might include a general proposal for the script, an outline of the events or scenes in the play, a sample scene, a first draft, a reading or workshop with actors, and a completed script with any revisions made.

A **monetary fee** for the total job should be agreed upon and included in the contract. Do some research on what the current market is for such a writing project. What are other local theatres paying for scripts of similar length? What do local writers think is a fair price? What are your granting agencies willing to allocate for fees to local artists? Don't hesitate to offer what you can even if it is lower than the going rate. Some writers will work for what you can afford to pay in order to have their work produced. Perhaps they can make up the difference in future royalties from other theatres. Be certain you have the funding before you sign a contract.

The contract should include a clear statement of who will retain the **copyright** to the script and what the **production rights** are for your theatre. For any script written for The Seasoned Performers, the writer holds the copyright and the theatre is allowed to perform the play at any time without royalty.

Do not guarantee to produce the commissioned script. Budget time for rewrites.

Using "Nonperformance" Material for Performing

Theatre productions are not always plays. Various kinds of literature can be performed as a very theatrical type of entertainment without having a normal play script at all. This concept can be useful when a special theatrical group finds itself lacking a suitable play to produce or when it simply wants to do something different for a change of pace.

Stories of all sorts can be staged, poetry and prose can be read, journals or letters can be brought to life in a reading. This kind of performance can be especially suitable for senior adults who may also enjoy the process of research and selection. Holidays, historical events, folklore, seasons, or celebrations may inspire the choice of certain material.

There is still the issue of copyright laws, which also apply to nonperformance material. Give yourself plenty of time and choose material that is in the public domain or for which you can secure rights.

Subject Matter

There are no real limits to the types of subject matter that can be explored by senior adults. Older theatre artists and audiences have a wealth of knowledge, history, culture, and interests. But whether you are selecting a written script, commissioning a play from a writer, planning to create a performance piece within the group, or selecting nonperformance material, it is wise to consider your particular actors and audiences.

What activities and lifestyles do your actors pursue? What issues involve them? Are you limited in numbers of actors available—especially male? Does your mission include education, entertainment, or any specific messages? What about the education level, age, and degree of sophistication of your audiences? Some senior theatres focus on the experience of aging as subject matter; others like to vary their options.

Subject matter should allow older adults to see themselves in a positive, up-to-date, and fully human way. Older characters can be involved with adventures, mysteries, life crises, issues, and interactions of all sorts. Senior adult actors don't have to be limited to roles of a certain age. They can play characters of any age in plays about history, legends, fantasies, memories, and so on. The style of the production can accommodate the actors.

. . .

Although it can be challenging to find or create good theatrical material for senior adults, it can also be one of the most creatively rewarding aspects of working in this field. Senior adult theatre is emerging as an entity worthy of attention. New plays are being created for this particular constituency, and as more theatres produce them there will be even more of these challenging and stimulating theatre pieces.

Other Programming

Creative Dramatics
Some senior adult theatre programs offer drama activities for older adults that do not result in a performance. Especially those programs associated with assisted-living

facilities, whose participants are very elderly, may choose to use this type of programming. Creative Dramatics techniques provide stimulating activities and interaction without the stresses associated with trying to produce a show.

Come, Step into My Life (1996), by Rosilyn Wilder (New Plays), describes Life Drama with youth and elders in a process that engages people of any age in dramatic play. Activities suggested in other Creative Dramatics texts can be adapted for use with senior adults.

Classes and Workshops

Often, senior adults want to learn and participate in theatre activities without the commitment of time for long rehearsal periods or the stresses of performance. Classes and workshops especially for older adults in acting, improvisation, comedy, etc. can fill this need. Some classes might involve "seeing theatre" productions and coming together for discussions and review. Some of these classes might serve as training grounds and recruitment sources for actors for the productions of a theatre, but they can also offer nonthreatening opportunities for the benefits that participation in the theatre can bring. Classes could be a source of revenue for the program.

Storytelling and Reading

Although full-scale productions may be done using traditions of storytelling or readers theatre, these forms can be appropriate for very informal performances and can suit a variety of venues. Scripts are held for readers theatre and stories can be read or told in the storyteller's own words. These formats eliminate the need for exact memorization of lines and have the advantage of being shows that can be held in readiness to be quickly polished when a performance opportunity arises. Rehearsals are needed for putting together these small-scale performances but do not require as extensive a time commitment. These can be alternative options in the programming of a senior adult theatre.

. . .

A senior adult theatre program does not have to produce plays in order to offer the benefits of theatre activity to its participants. There may be reasons for your particular group to choose alternative programming alone, or you may want to add it to round out a complete theatre curriculum. These activities can enrich a senior adult theatre program of any size, can add to the quality of all the productions, and can attract more participants who are reluctant to engage in traditional performance theatre.

5

Space and Technical Matters

When The Seasoned Performers first began, the group was shuffled around in a senior center, from a conference room to a library room, even briefly occupying a large closet—and borrowing cast-off vans to tour to performance sites. When members finally managed to find a Sunday school classroom for rehearsals and a shared office with their own telephone, typewriter, and filing cabinet, they were in business! This is not to suggest that this is the best way to start—only to show that theatre can be done with minimal space and equipment, if necessary, and that you can grow toward something more adequate.

If it falls to you to find space for your senior adult theatre, this chapter offers guidance for analyzing your needs and locating an appropriate and adequate space. It also addresses technical support and other equipment needs that you may have.

Begin by analyzing your programming goals to pinpoint just what your needs will be in these respects: Will you need a large space for a group to rehearse, have production meetings, and/or hold workshops and classes? Will you require another space for building sets and making costumes, another for office work, and yet another for storage?

You may be sharing, renting, or borrowing a theatre for your performances or you may simply convert your rehearsal room into a "theatre." You may be touring your performances to whatever space is offered at various community sites.

You might decide that you need your own theatrical equipment, such as lighting and sound, or you may borrow or rent these items. Of course you may determine that your particular theatre troupe won't require these trappings at all.

Will you keep any of the set pieces, props, and costumes for future use? Where will you keep them and any equipment that is not in active use?

What specific work needs to be handled in an office? Will you be sharing office space and equipment, or will you have your own?

Space Considerations

The physical limitations and psychological welfare of your participants and your audiences are important factors as well as the adequacy of a space for your senior adult theatre. Accessibility and safety are two main concerns when choosing a place for seniors to work. This begins with the general location. The space should be located in an area of town where older adults feel safe and comfortable. The facility should be well-maintained and attractive. All external areas should be well-lit. Parking should be near an entrance with handicapped access. If public transportation is a factor, the proximity of access should be considered.

Elevators should be available if the work space is not located on a ground-floor level. Any stairways should have handrails, and steps should be finished with nonslip treads and contrasting edges. All spaces should be well-lit, including entrances, hallways, and rest rooms as well as work areas. Work areas should be equipped with temperature control, be clean and open, and have comfortable seating available. Avoid slippery rugs and any sudden changes in the floor that may cause tripping. Rest rooms and water fountains should be easily accessible and near the areas you are using.

Rehearsal/Workshop Space

In searching for a large, comfortable space that is private and quiet and has an open area and some seating available for rehearsals or theatre workshops, remember that timing is sometimes key. If you hold your activities at times other than when a community facility is needed for its primary use, then perhaps your group may use the space for free or for a minimum charge. Some groups have bartered for space, offering a performance or workshop in return for rehearsal time. Others have arranged to give a percentage of their ticket sales receipts to the facility.

Begin by looking at community school and college locations, churches, senior centers, community recreation facilities, and theatres. Often, these facilities are very busy at certain times, but if you are working during weekdays or very early evenings, or during some other time of the year, the space may be available. These types of entities may want to serve more of the community or may want to attract more senior adults and, therefore, may be open to your group working there on a regular basis or periodically.

Performance Space

Theatres' spaces can present special problems when used by older actors and audiences. Traditionally, there are many darkened areas in the house and most especially backstage. Older eyes do not adjust as quickly nor as thoroughly as younger eyes and may not be able to distinguish edges and surfaces with as much depth perception. An actor moving from a brightly lit dressing room to a darkened backstage area to a very brightly lit stage may experience discomfort and disorientation, which may lead to accidents or missed cues. Dressing rooms are sometimes located a long distance from the stage or even on a different level. This could be an obstacle for actors who may move slower or with difficulty.

With some planning and modification, these problems can be lessened and real theatres can be successfully utilized for senior adults. Perhaps you could set up dressing room areas closer to the stage. You could add more "stumble lights" and glow-tape backstage. You could use additional offstage assistants for guiding actors to their "places" and give actors more time to move from place to place. The company could make scene changes in a "glow" rather than a full blackout. All wiring across floors should be completely secured with strong tape, and objects that could be barriers or cause stumbling should be moved or clearly marked. You could use an amplified communications system to allow the actors to hear their cues more easily. The theatre entrance should be made handicapped-accessible for audience members. Using the brightest setting on the house lights could be helpful, and additional ushers could be assigned to escort those who need help moving down aisles to their seats—and back up the aisles at intermissions and after the show.

In order to avoid some of these problems altogether, to save the expenses involved in using a theatre space, to serve your particular constituency, or to reach more senior adult audiences, you may decide to do your performances in a nontraditional theatre space. This could be an activity room in a community center or church, a small auditorium in a public or private building, a dining room in a residential facility, even a classroom. All that is really required is enough space to perform, space for the audience to sit, and enough lighting for the audience to see the actors. You may, of course, elect to bring in more light-ing as well as your sets, sound equipment, props, and actors. Or you may accept the space as it is, only rear-ranging enough to accommodate the audience and your production. This could very well be the same space in which you have rehearsed, saving your actors the stress of moving the production to a different location.

Office Space

In the beginning, it may seem that any little "cubby" will do for the amount of office work you intend. However, as your theatre grows, you will invariably need more space. As the theatre matures, you will probably have more equipment, more staff, and more records to store. It is use-ful to anticipate these needs from the start so you can begin targeting the appropriate office space.

For an office that is fully supportive of a theatre program, you should plan enough space for a desk or two, plus space for a computer, monitor, and printer, several storage and file cabinets, a copy machine, telephone(s), answering and fax machines, a typing table, a work table, and extra seat-ing. These needs will vary with each theatre program.

It would be ideal for this office space to be in the same facility as the rehearsal space, but this is not absolutely necessary nor always possible. You may be offered free rehearsal space in a facility that won't have the kind of office space you need. Try to keep office and rehearsal space at least near each other so that quick trips can be made when necessary.

Sharing office space with another entity is a possibility that can work if there is sufficient area or if different schedules can be arranged so that your staff can have pri-vacy. This situation, although not ideal, can allow your theatre to grow to a point where it can afford to pay rent or can locate its own space.

Again, you will need to consider accessibility and safety factors in locating the office as well as certain equipment accommodations for older adults. Even if you have a younger staff, older participants may be using or helping in the office at some time, and you may want to make a special effort to employ older staff members or volunteers in the office.

Storage Space

The first storage need to consider is where you will keep the properties and other items needed during the rehearsal process if the rehearsal space is used for other activities. A secure closet area in the room or nearby or a large storage unit could prevent the necessity of hauling things in and out for every rehearsal during this extended time. Most rehearsals require at least a few props, and you may be adding furniture or other set pieces by the end of the process. Remember this need when locating your rehearsal space.

You should also consider ongoing storage needs for permanent belongings. Theatres tend to acquire an amazing assortment of properties, costumes, and set pieces over a period of time. Even if you borrow most things and intend to return them or if you give away or discard accumulations at the end of every production, there will likely be some items that you will decide to keep for the future. Even the most minimal theatrical equipment should be kept in a secure and protected place while not in use.

If your theatre controls a large enough space, perhaps part of it can be utilized for storage. Certainly on-site storage is best. You may be sharing storage space with a larger theatre, or perhaps putting theatrical things in someone's basement or garage, or renting a ministorage unit. These areas should be easily accessible, have adequate lighting, have temperature and moisture control, and have low shelving for use by older adults. Everything in storage should be clearly labeled and marked for identification. Keep an up-to-date inventory of stored items and check them regularly.

Technical Considerations

Equipment

Senior adult theatres are generally relatively small units with relatively small budgets. If yours is a part of a larger whole, perhaps you have a fully equipped theatre that you may use. If not, you may be starting with minimal equipment or borrowing or renting as you have the need.

Besides budgetary considerations, keep in mind that the size and weight of equipment, the ladders, rigging, catwalks, and other theatrical paraphernalia can be dangerous when used by people with physical limitations. Whether your theatre has personnel able to handle the equipment may define in part what you will acquire or use in your productions. The style and type of productions you will do is another consideration.

Sound equipment is perhaps the most beneficial type of electronic accessory for a senior adult theatre. Amplification of actors' voices is a need not only for audiences with impaired hearing but for actors with aging voices that may no longer have adequate power. Also, music and sound effects can enhance productions. Basic equipment may include body microphones and/or other types of microphones and stands, speakers and speaker stands, a cassette deck, a CD player, a sound-mixer board, an amplifier, and various cables and adapters.

This amount of equipment could cost thousands of dollars but may be acquired in stages over a period of time, and it also may be possible to rent the items you need. A nearby college or university theatre department or a community theatre would be able to direct you to a vendor for this equipment in your area where a consultant can guide you to the items that best suit your needs. The weight of some of this equipment varies widely, as does the power. Consider the amount of space you will fill as well as the people who will be handling the equipment.

Lighting equipment is another resource for which senior adult theatres may lack the budgets and physical abilities. Real theatre stages require some theatrical lighting so the audience can see the actors. In other performance spaces, available lighting may be sufficient or additional lighting may enhance the theatrical look of a show. The company will have to make choices depending on style of production, budgets, and other resources.

It is important to work with whatever technical equipment you choose to use with enough time to adjust for any problems that the equipment may cause. For instance, the heat and glare of lights may affect the actors, or putting on a body microphone may take assistance and extra time.

Sets, Costumes, and Properties

Most of the plays now being written specifically for senior adult theatre require only very simple settings, costumes, and props, recognizing the budget and physical restrictions usually associated with these organizations. Most plays can be modified in production style to accommodate the limitations of a theatre troupe. However, many groups would like to enhance their productions with as much of the visual elements of theatre as possible, since this can add so much to the overall effectiveness of the show. For mature actors, it is necessary to consider the requirements of *using* the set, costumes, and props as much as taking into account the budget and creation of these aspects of the production.

The general design of a setting for use by older actors should take into account possible physical limitations such as movement restrictions and changes in eyesight. Leaders should consider accommodations such as:

1. use of visual contrast in the settings
2. elimination of platforms, steps, or area rugs
3. restrictions in the size of the stage area used by the actors
4. avoidance of chairs or other seating that is too low—or soft—or too high (Chairs with arms may assist an actor in rising. If you use stools, choose a twenty-four-inch height rather than a thirty-inch one.)
5. simplification or avoidance of set pieces or props that work in complex ways

Choice of materials for set pieces will be based on considerations such as expense, durability, strength and weight, ease of handling, safety, and whether the production will tour or need to be moved. You may choose light-weight, inexpensive goods such as foam core—which will not hold up for very long and tends to warp—fabric, and aluminum over plywood, fiberglass, and other metals, for instance. Durability and portability of materials are more important considerations for a tour than for a play that only runs for a few performances in one place. (See the section on touring later in this chapter.)

Properties, the smaller articles and objects on the set that may be handled by the actors, are subject to similar considerations as the larger settings. They may be constructed, borrowed, or bought specifically for the production. Avoid heavy, bulky, or otherwise hard-to-handle pieces. Properties should be provided early in the rehearsal process so that the actors can practice using them.

Costumes for a play may be constructed, rented from

costume houses, borrowed from friends, bought from thrift shops or other stores, or chosen from items in the actors' own closets. Often, the addition of a simple accessory such as a hat, scarf, or jewelry over a basic outfit can complete a transformation into a character. This can also add to the fun of the process for the cast and crew. You will need to consider the resources of the troupe and the organization.

The costumes should be designed to allow for safety of movement, avoiding overly bulky, heavy, or long items. Remember that the actor may not be able to work without glasses and these will have to be accepted.

Costumes changes during a performance can be hazardous. If they are necessary, the changes should involve a minimum of items. Changing a jacket or accessory may be much wiser than an entire outfit. It may be a good idea to provide a helper offstage for even the simplest of changes. Avoid things that must be put on over the head. Extra rehearsal time should be provided for costume changes as well as practice in working in costumes.

The Seasoned Performers troupe has simplified productions over the years in the use of costumes, more and more using the actors' own clothing and only constructing or buying specialty costumes. However, some productions have been particularly rewarding because of the creativity involved in making the costumes.

Getting It Done

The resources of a theatre will define some of the solutions for accomplishing the technical requirements of a production. Do you have access to adequate space and equipment for building a set, props, and costumes? Do you have a technical associate who can plan and oversee set and prop building and finding and the setting up and running of any equipment? Is there budget to hire a temporary technician to handle any heavy and skilled work? Do you have an experienced volunteer willing and able to serve as a supervisor? Do you have access to enough volunteers for the work to be done? Is there enough youthful muscle and dexterity for jobs that require them? The availability of personnel to carry out and oversee the technical aspects of a production will dictate the scope of your plans.

One of the most satisfying features of volunteering in a theatre can be in putting one's creative skills to work or in learning new skills. An organized and guided process in achieving these aspects of a production is important. Working in groups can be particularly rewarding to older adults, and, especially given an adequate amount of time and guidance, the results can be remarkably satisfying. But, if circumstances restrict the necessary personnel— whether volunteer or staff—in organizing, leading, and carrying out these projects, you should make plans for a simpler production.

The talents of older artists and artisans should be used and celebrated in senior adult theatre. Check into the possibility of getting help from senior adults from art associations, sewing or woodworking guilds, and other such organizations when a production requires special skills. However, senior adult theatre does not necessarily rule out assistance by younger volunteers or staff. Technical assistance may come from families, students at nearby high schools or colleges, or technicians from local theatres, performance arenas, or electronic businesses.

Touring

Some senior adult theatres tour their plays in order to reach more audiences and to bring live theatre to groups who could not ordinarily attend productions. This may require transportation for the actors and supporting personnel and certainly for any equipment, sets, furnishings, properties, and costumes used in the production. If transportation for senior adults is a vehicle such as a van, it should be equipped with a pull-down step for ease in getting on and off. For any but the very simplest productions, a driver/technician is probably a necessity for touring. Portable rolling carts and hand trucks may be needed for maneuvering heavy pieces into the playing space. Other indispensable touring items may include a cell phone, a first-aid kit, toolboxes, a folding table, a costume repair kit, an iron, many rolls of strong tape, large golf umbrellas, maps, a flashlight, and a list of emergency numbers.

Gather as much information about the performance space as possible before arriving with the production. See the performance area beforehand, preferably, whether you are touring to a theatre or nontheatrical space. Speak to technicians or someone familiar with the space and equipment. Find out where you will unload and whether you can use any of the house systems for sound and lighting. Make sure that the space will be cleared for you before you arrive. Arrange for any help that you will need.

Touring and performing in nontheatrical spaces brings special technical considerations in designing an environment for the play. Will you accept the available lighting and acoustics, or will you bring equipment? Will you accept the background of the room as that of the play with a few added small pieces such as lightweight chairs and tables? Will you set up flats or any set units as scenery? Will you be able to have any "backstage" space for entrances or for the actors to await their cues?

A theatre designer or technician may be able to custom design a lightweight, portable set especially for a touring show. The Seasoned Performers troupe has adapted a display unit made of aluminum tubing designed to fit together to stand and support a fabric backdrop. This "set" fits into a lightweight bag that can be carried in one hand. The painted backdrop provides not only a semblance of the setting for the audience but a "backstage" area for the actors. These units can be found in display showrooms or catalogs. The initial investment in a system of this kind can be large, but such a unit can be used again and again with different backdrops.

.   .   .

The space and technical considerations of a theatre can vary widely according to budgets, resources, and scope of productions. With planning and ingenuity these need not be stumbling blocks in building a program. As with every area of a senior adult theatre, limitations can aid in creativity, helping you focus on solutions that can define style and scope. Whether you are working in a fully equipped theatre or an ordinary activity space with no theatrical accoutrements, effective theatre productions can be enjoyed by the audiences and participants in your senior adult theatre.

6

Marketing

If pouring your heart and soul and sometimes blood, sweat, and tears into a production or program is not pain enough, you then have to *sell* the product. Actually, this aspect of theatre can be creatively satisfying and fun as well as helpful in paying the bills.

A significant element of a senior adult theatre no matter what the size of the community to be reached, marketing can not only influence the numbers of audience members who are attracted to performances but can affect funding potential and attract participants as well. Marketing is used not only to sell tickets but to sell an image of the theatre. Potential audience, supporters, donors, and participants respond to the image the company presents. The publicizing of a single event also helps to market future events and activities of a theatre. Planning and budgeting should be made for this aspect of a theatre program whether you are working with a full-fledged marketing campaign or are simply trying to get residents of a facility to make the effort to come downstairs and see a performance.

Even if a theatre only expects to take advantage of "free" marketing opportunities such as posting announcements in a residential or other facility, press releases in newspapers, or personal appearances at meetings or on local television or radio talk shows, there will be costs involved. The time for creating articles and flyers, the costs of artwork, typing and printing, stationery and envelopes, photographs, and telephone/fax or e-mail will all be part of the budget for marketing.

Naming Your Senior Adult Theatre

One of the most important marketing decisions is made during the very beginning stages of a senior adult theatre—the name. This name can speak volumes about who you are, what you do, what your spirit and attitude may be, and whether someone would want to see your work or join your group. It will be the first element in creating your identity and building your image.

Many senior adult theatre programs and companies cleverly combine the idea of being older with some idea pertaining to theatre. This can result in fun and appealing names that clearly define the theatre company, such as Curtain Time Retirement Vignettes; the Extended Run Players; the Ripe and Ready Players; the Slightly Older Adult Players (SOAP), which produces "squeaky clean entertainment"; and Stagebridge, which aims to bridge the generation gap through theatrical endeavors.

Analyzing Your Market

Although you may want a general audience for your senior adult theatre, there may be some specific population segments that you especially want to reach. Begin by finding the answers to pertinent questions about your goals and target groups:

1. Does your mission include reaching special segments of the population with your programming? What are the sizes of the populations to be reached?
2. Who are the potential supporters of your program?

3. Where do these people live? Where do they go and what do they do? What are their interests, their level of education?
4. What media reach and influence them?
5. Will you be selling to groups as well as to individuals?

The more informed you are, the more effective you can be in making your marketing efforts count. The local chamber of commerce and area agency on aging may be able to help with this analysis, as will individuals working with the special populations you are trying to reach.

Direct Contact

The more direct your contact with individuals, the more likely you are to influence them. This includes in-person endeavors, direct mailers and other printed materials, and telephone calls. Budgeting time as well as money is necessary for these activities, and you will have to decide how best to use these resources. You may be able to reach more people with direct mailers than either personal visits to groups or telephone calls to individuals. Still, sending a few actors to preview a "bit" for a large church group, for instance, can whet the appetite and motivate people to buy tickets and come to a performance.

Telephone calls can be most effective when used as a follow-up reminder after other publicity has been distributed. After press releases and feature articles have appeared in the media and/or flyers have been sent or posted, a personal telephone call can yield tangible results such as tickets being sold, reservations made, or performances booked. To conserve time and make the most of this effort, you may narrow the field a bit by choosing a list of activities directors, leaders of senior adult groups, regular supporters, or new prospects to receive calls.

The Mailing List

One of the most commonly used marketing tools in theatre is a mailer to individuals on a list. With senior theatre, a mailing list might include activities directors of groups, clubs, and retirement communities as well as other individuals. The list should include members of funding agencies, government officials, and other supporters as well as those to whom you wish to sell the performances. It will take time to develop a good mailing list. You may start with lists that you can get from other theatre groups or arts agencies, from civic clubs, churches, or area agencies on aging. These may be free of charge, although some organizations market their list for a fee—and some may not want to share it at all. You may ask audience members to sign a mailing list as they attend the theatre. Your participants can contribute to your list. Gradually, you can hone your list into a manageable and effective one designed for your theatre.

Keeping the mailing list up-to-date and free of duplicate names is an essential and ongoing task if a list is to be effective. Each time a large mailing is sent, there will be some pieces that are returned with address changes or marked "unknown." Try to make these corrections in your list as soon as possible. Each time new additions are made to the list, check it by sorting alphabetically and removing any duplications.

This, of course, assumes the list is kept in a computer database, from which labels or envelopes can be printed, letters can be personalized, a variety of sorting options achieved, and statistics kept. Assigning a "type"—such as club, retirement community, school, arts agency, government, etc.—to each listing in a database offers the possibility of selecting specific groups of names to receive mailings.

Mailers

With a direct mailing, you may be attracting an audience for a show, selling season tickets, marketing a tour, announcing other events, recruiting participants, or requesting special support for the theatre. The mailer may be simple or a more detailed, complex packet. Be specific in how you want your recipients to respond. People should know how they will benefit from taking the desired action. Try to motivate them to move quickly.

Only a certain percentage of your mailings will get a response. To make the mailer as effective as possible, be concise and clear in your information and use attractive artwork and design. Whether the mailer is created by hand, on a computer, or designed and executed by a professional print shop or advertising agency, it should reflect the overall image of your theatre.

It is best to use a first-class stamp for the mailer. Bulk-mailing rates can be cheaper if a large number of items are sent, but the rules for this are complicated and many people simply throw away bulk mailings without reading them.

The timing of a mailer can be crucial to the response. Sent too long in advance, the information can be forgotten or lost. On the other hand, recipients may not be able to move quickly enough when a mailer is sent at the last minute. For most productions or special events, two to three weeks in advance will be sufficient time for people to make their plans to attend and to make reservations if needed. If you are selling season tickets, a month to three months before the first production will be ample time for subscribers to respond. For touring productions that have schedules and arrangements to be made in advance, a mailer sent out at least two months in advance may be needed. Try to give recipients at least a month to make plans when you are advertising a workshop. In all of these cases, there will be time for follow-up telephone calls to a select list, should you choose to make them.

These mailers will be not only for selling your production; they can let contributors and supporters—both active and potential—know about the activities of your program.

Flyers

A good flyer should contain:

1. Who?—the name of the theatre and the supporting entities
2. What?—the name of the production(s) or event
3. Where and When?—the location and time
4. Why?—the benefits and attractions
5. How much?—the price
6. How?—how to make reservations, buy a ticket, or sign up

The flyer should also contain an attention-getting, attractive design. People are subjected to many computer-generated flyers on the same familiar colors of paper every day. Unique choices of clipart, original art, photographs, layout, shape, colors, materials, and wording can set your flyer apart from the rest and command the desired attention. Make sure that the lettering you use is large enough and easily legible and that the design is not so complex as to be confusing. Try to keep the message simple and use as much "white" or blank space as possible for clarity. Especially for older eyes, the printing should be of contrasting color to the background.

"Copy-ready" material can be quickly and easily reproduced on any color paper on a copier or at a copy shop. For more complicated jobs such as full-color prints and material that must be typeset, the work can be done at a full-service print shop. *Note:* Printing might be available in-kind from a sympathetic print shop.

You may create a flyer that will be used in a mailer and which can also be posted on bulletin boards, hallways, storefront windows, etc. With a larger budget, the flyer may be enlarged on more durable paper for posters, and it may be used for a printed advertisement in a newspaper or other publication. A similar design may then be used on a printed program. Keep these different usages in mind when deciding upon flyer design. This repetition of a single design can reinforce the image of the show and make it more memorable.

This idea of image reinforcement can be utilized in marketing a theatre with the design of a logo, an identifying symbol of an entity that may include the name. A theatre can use its logo on most of its printed materials.

Letterhead Stationery and Business Cards

Once your theatre is ready to do any type of correspondence, letterhead stationery is needed. This is an effective marketing tool, verifying the business, giving important information, establishing an image of the theatre, and reinforcing this image each time the stationery is seen. The headings can be produced by a computer and printed on your choice of stationery and envelopes, or a full-service printing company can assist with this process and produce a very polished look.

The stationery should contain the name, address, and telephone number of the theatre. Other information, such as purpose, affiliations, and board of directors may be given. The envelope should bear the name and address of the theatre.

Business cards may also be printed with suitable information. These are very handy for inclusion in a packet or for giving information to interested parties and can be distributed among all the participants to hand out for effective marketing.

Brochures

One of the most useful printed items for spreading the word about a theatre is a well-designed brochure. These can be included in a larger mailer or you can design them to be mailed themselves. You can place them in brochure racks or on information tables for distribution in many different venues. They can be included in packets such as those sent to media or newcomers or distributed at conventions. You can simply hand them to anyone wanting information on the program.

A brochure will be more general in its description of the theatre so that it can be used over a longer period of time than a flyer, which describes specific events. It can include information on purposes, programming, participants, and support. It can include photographs or other artwork to help define and sell the program. It can be a platform for proclaiming the benefits and rewards for audiences and participants in the theatre.

Costs can vary widely with the design and production choices. Assistance in designing a brochure can be found in desktop publishing software, a printing service, or an advertising agency.

Newsletters

A newsletter is a means of keeping groups of people informed about current and upcoming activities and productions, noteworthy stories, and other items of interest. They may be utilized for communicating with participants but may also be useful in informing season ticket holders, supporters, and prospective parties about offerings and accomplishments of the theatre.

Newsletters are often especially useful for senior adult

programs since the theatre may not be in the "main-stream" of an area's arts and entertainment scene. The content can help to inform more of the general public and potential supporters about the activities and accomplishments of a very special theatre.

Newsletters can be in the form of a very simple letter or can achieve a more traditional look with headings, columns, and clipart with the use of a desktop publishing computer program. You can design them to be mailed as a single piece or included in a larger mailer.

Photographs

One of the best ways to give an accurate image of the special nature of senior adult theatre is with actual photographs of the actors and audiences involved. These photographs can be sent to publications such as newspapers or arts newsletters, reproduced in printed materials such as brochures and flyers, used to create albums, slide shows, and display boards, and used by the theatre and individuals to keep a record of activities. There is little question that photographs are one of the most effective means of communicating about and marketing a theatre program or production.

Color prints and slides and black-and-white photographs are all useful to have on hand for unexpected opportunities and planned marketing. Some publications may request that you provide them with a usable picture. Most will prefer to use a slide or black-and-white photograph, but some will use a color print if the contrast is good.

Newspapers may prefer to take their own photographs but could use yours, especially if you provide them with a good black-and-white print. For most newspapers, a close, action shot of no more than three to four people is desirable for clarity. Choose an image with good contrast and simple backgrounds. Tape a note to the back of each photograph giving information such as the name of theatre, production, and individuals in the picture and the photographer's name. Do not write on the photograph itself, as the print may come through and ruin the picture.

When pictures are taken, be sure to include shots of the entire set and some that document costumes as well as closer action shots with several people involved and some close-up shots of actors' faces. Take several angles of your compositions. This will raise your odds of getting some excellent pictures and ensure that you have a variety of photographs from which to choose. Try to get pictures of everyone involved, including the technical people doing their jobs.

Be sure to keep your photographs and negatives organized and use proper storage to ensure their preservation. Keep several reprints on hand of especially good photographs.

Press Packets

So called because this type of portfolio is often given to members of the press to use for material in a news or feature article, a press packet can also be useful for other marketing opportunities when you want to give a full picture of your theatre program. It is a flexible folder with several pockets for printed items and slits for a business card, which can hold a brochure, perhaps a newsletter and other information sheets, photocopies of clippings and articles, photographs, and current flyers and programs. This pulls together all of a theatre's printed marketing materials into one easily handled unit. Items can be added or deleted as events change or as the purpose dictates.

You can have packs of this sort professionally designed and produced by advertising agencies or printing services, or you can simply put them together in a packet obtained at an office supply store, adding an identifying label to the outside to personalize the unit. Arts councils may be able to provide a technical assistance grant for a professional portfolio.

Display

Opportunities for personal contact or exhibits at senior fairs, theatre conferences, and other public events can make your program more visible and introduce your theatre to more people. These can also be occasions for networking with other exhibitors, which may be beneficial. In all cases, you will need to judge whether the exposure will be worth the time and expense involved.

Often, these display areas consist of a table with a few chairs or just an empty space that you can fill as you like. You may simply need a standing sign and a few brochures, or you may need a more elaborate setup including a folding table with a cover and a backdrop or easel for photographs and signs. You may have a portable slide show available. Suitable equipment may be purchased from a display company, or you can make your own simple display units. A presentation can be made of two or more small wooden-framed bulletin boards hinged together to make a standing screen on which photos and other material can be tacked.

Usually the display will need to be manned during certain hours, but in some situations, the exhibit can be set up and left. You may choose to have actors in costume meeting and greeting people. The more eye-catching, personal, and fun your display, the more people will notice and remember it. Try to anticipate questions and have answers and printed material ready to hand out. Find out how you will get the exhibit in and out of the space.

Internet Web Sites

More and more people, including senior adults, are utilizing technology for giving and receiving information. One of the fastest-growing opportunities for networking and research is the Internet. This can be expensive and time-consuming to learn but can definitely be worth the investment for a theatre.

Some senior adult theatres have their own Web site that gives information on shows and classes, sells tickets, or takes bookings. Some states and arts organizations offer Web space within their sites for small arts groups to give information.

The Web is also a good way to connect to information on other senior theatres, performance material, books, conferences, funding, etc. that can expand the potential of a theatre program. (See Appendix II.)

Senior Theatre Connections (*www.seniortheatre.com*) is a networking link for senior adult theatres and offers a way to market a program. A printed directory by Bonnie L. Vorenberg is available, also called *Senior Theatre Connections* (ArtAge Publications), highlighting performers, groups, and individuals who work in senior arts and listing many helpful resources.

Printed Programs

Not only can printed programs give information on the play, the production, the cast and crew, and supporters, but they can be opportunities for marketing future productions and development, workshops, and ways to work with or support the program. Space for advertising can be sold to offset some of the printing cost.

Again, it is very important that printing be large enough for older eyes to read easily. If you have so much information that it begins to look crowded, consider adding more pages to the program.

Proofread the program—and all printed material—several times. It is helpful to have several people proofread material. And always check the actual size of printing before copying or printing is done. Sometimes words will look different on a computer screen than on the actual printed page. Reductions made to fit a space can turn out so small that no one can read them.

Other Methods

T-Shirts and Other Paraphernalia

Special T-shirts and other items such as caps, tote bags, mugs, and pens can be useful advertising as well as fun souvenirs for participants and audience members of an individual production or a theatre. Some of these items can be especially attention-getting and can bring about opportunities for telling people about a show or theatre program.

A few participants wearing T-shirts can make a memorable impression when talking to groups about their show. Public appearances of this sort can be fun as well as productive in attracting audiences or other participants.

The image of the logo or a flyer design from an individual show may be effectively used for a T-shirt and can be easily reproduced by a custom screen-printing company. The printing company may have or recommend an artist to assist if special artwork is desired.

Signs

Another opportunity for getting the theatre's name into the public's eye is through signage. Whether you have use of a marquee or have to use a temporary sign posted at the entrance to a performance space, this written image of your name is important. Try to make the best use of any occasion to post a sign. This includes any vehicle used by the theatre, doors of offices, rehearsal or performance spaces, and exhibits. If you have a logo, it can be reproduced on the signs.

Videotaping

A videotape of a production or a workshop event not only preserves the history of a theatre and may serve as a learning tool but can be used in marketing, public relations, and fund-raising. A good video can serve as proof of the quality of productions and can effectively show the people who are involved. The company can use a video when seeking funding from a corporation or a funding agency and when recruiting new participants for the program. Videotaping a script requires special permission unless the group owns *all* right to it. License to perform isn't license to tape, even by amateurs.

The best videos are done under professional conditions with proper background and lighting by an experienced cameraperson, but some very acceptable tapes can be made by an amateur with a video camera on a tripod during a performance. Try to get duplicates made and protect the tape from being recorded over. Use suitable storage and organization methods for these tapes so that they are ready when you need to use them.

Media

Television and radio stations are required by the Federal Communications Commission to offer time for public-service announcements and will usually read information sent to them for items of interest to the community. Some stations have live interview programs for community-interest features or sections of a newscast for such material. Newspapers also have space devoted to announcements of these events and related feature articles or human-interest stories. Check with editors of the arts, lifestyle, social, neighborhood, or similar sections of the newspaper. Some cities have magazines and other publications that give opportunities to print these items. Find out what your community offers in the way of this free advertising. Call the program managers of television and radio stations and the editors of appropriate sections of newspapers and other periodicals for information. Some publications will have this information in print near the desired section.

The stations and publications will have different deadlines and procedures, so it is important to learn what rules apply. Keep a written record of these procedures and the contact people at each place. Try to establish personal contact with the people in charge of these areas of the media. They can tell you the preferred formats, and you might suggest an interview, photograph, or feature article to be released before the opening of a show or other event.

For a live or taped interview, send your most personable and knowledgeable people armed with what facts to give, a good story, and one good statistic. For television, a colorful costume or prop can be effective. Avoid wearing checks, patterns, and white.

If you have the budget, a printed advertisement in a publication can be quite effective in reaching the public. Copy-ready material can be prepared by a computer or artist to be presented to the publication. Some newspapers have artists available to help for an extra charge. Publications especially for senior adults are usually less expensive for purchasing space than a larger newspaper and may be effective marketing choices for printed advertising.

Press Releases

Press releases are informational items that individual groups write themselves and send to newspapers, other periodicals, and radio and television stations. In general, a good press release is concise, giving the pertinent facts—

who, what, where, when, why, how and how much, who to contact and how—plus additional interesting information that may or may not be used. At the top of your typed page, put the name of the theatre and the specific subject along with a release date. The body of the article should be double-spaced, with the nonessential information at the end. At the very bottom of the page in parentheses, put the name and a telephone number of the person whom the station or paper can contact for more information.

Limit releases for radio and television spots to material that can be read in thirty seconds or less, and try to limit releases for newspapers to one typed page in length, if possible. For longer articles, the paper may have someone on staff write a feature or longer news story.

A Marketing Campaign

Marketing should not be left to chance or to those rare moments when there is nothing left to do on the production. Success of individual events, funding campaigns, and overall development depend on successful marketing. It should be a part of any long- and short-range planning and a strategic part of the overall program.

Time lines and deadlines for marketing should be made just as rehearsal, performing, and class schedules are made. Individual tasks should be specified and placed into these time lines, and when accomplished, evaluations should be made so that future marketing campaigns can be more effective.

Begin a marketing plan for a season by pinpointing the events to be marketed, fund-raising efforts, and other goals. Decide what creative strategies, promotions, and communications are needed for each of these pinpointed areas. You may see where one goal will affect another and efforts can be combined. Define the large tasks involved and fit them into a time line, then break these into smaller tasks with specific deadlines within that time line. An example of this process follows. It schedules a simple marketing plan for a touring play. This includes:

1. auditions announced—January 9–12
2. a mailer to three hundred individuals announcing availability of touring production—February 1
3. press releases to fifteen publications and six radio and TV stations—February 6–13
4. follow-up telephone calls to select individuals on mailing list—February 15–29
5. features (stories and interviews)—March 26–31
6. a mailer that includes a schedule of the tour sent to one hundred VIPs—March 27
7. a printed program mailed to touring sites for copying—March 20–May 10
8. T-shirts for company distributed—March 31
9. additional publicity during tour—April–May

The following calendar sets deadlines for tasks which ensure that the major marketing plan is effectively accomplished.

TOUR: APRIL 3–MAY 31

December

   1—audition flyer designed and proofed
   6—volunteer workdays organized for December through February
   10—audition flyer printed
   18—audition flyer mailed to groups
   19—audition press release written
   24–26—holidays
   27—audition press releases faxed or mailed to media

January

3—audition flyer posted in facilities

5—letter for mailer typed and proofed

7—production flyer for mailer designed and proofed

9–12—audition notices and announcements given in media

11—tour-availability press releases written

13—flyer and letter printed

14—press packet updated

17—envelopes for mailer addressed

18—evaluate effectiveness of marketing auditions

21—envelopes or fax covers for press packets and releases completed

24–28—press packets for media mailed (individual targeted dates)

26–28—media representatives contacted (features and interviews set up)

31—mailer packaged (flyer and letter added, envelopes stamped and sealed)

February

1—mailer sent

6–13—press releases published in media

15–29—follow-up telephone calls made to prospective sites

15—screen printers contacted for T-shirts

18—follow-up media contacts made

28—T-shirt designed

March

1–17—interviews given for publication features

3—T-shirt design sent to screen printers

6—newsletter for VIP mailer typed and proofed

10—newsletter printed

13—information gathered for printed program

15—layout designed for program

17—typing completed for program

17—bookings completed

18—evaluate effectiveness of marketing tour

20–May 10—program copy distributed to sites for printing

21–31—live interviews given

24—printed schedules and newsletter added to VIP mailer

24—T-shirts completed

27—mailer sent to VIP's

31—T-shirts distributed to company

April

10—color and black-and-white show photographs taken

14—updated press releases typed and proofed

21—updated press packets with photos sent to select publications

27—show videotaped

May

8—TV coverage of tour/interview provided

June

5—evaluate effectiveness of overall marketing and touring production

Even a simple marketing plan can seem overwhelming unless you create adequate planning and scheduling. When this yearlong plan is completed in advance, not only can you adjust the plan for the realities of budget and for staff and volunteer time, but you might also combine marketing efforts to accomplish several goals. In the previoues example, the extra mailer to VIPs is part of an overall plan to develop fund-raising potential. This uses the flyer describing the production, the touring schedule, and an overall program update in the newsletter to give the theatre's image a boost with key people. The large mailer and the feature articles might also be used to publicize several planned events for the year and to recruit more participants as well as to interest audiences in the touring production.

Even with the most careful planning, there may be glitches in the publicity. You will not always be able to get the media coverage that you wish. Two feature stories in a row, for example, is unlikely. Mistakes or delays that you cannot control may be made by any of the many services you use. Remember not to schedule tasks too tightly and try to do a variety of marketing efforts so you are not completely ruined by someone else's mistake.

. . .

For creative people who rather like being in the limelight, marketing can be a fun and productive part of the theatre experience. A healthy marketing plan can do much to enhance the growth of a theatre. The special qualities of a senior adult theatre can attract attention with the media and public. The people involved, the specific subject matter, and the programming done by a senior adult theatre are all attractive material for human-interest and arts-related stories. Be prepared when the opportunities arise for telling your story. Keep making the opportunities arise.

7

Managing the Office

Theatre is a business—a creative business and, in the case of a senior adult theatre, sometimes an especially delicate business. A smoothly run, efficient office is particularly important for a senior adult theatre. It is a place where not only are the programs organized and sustained, but crises are managed and volunteers are coordinated and supported. The office is a key factor in making sure that stresses which may arise don't become overwhelming.

The office chores will involve planning, training, communications, and record keeping for events, marketing, fund-raising, and financial and legal obligations. It may include design and artwork as well as more usual office functions. As with other areas of senior adult theatre, the type of structure will dictate whether the office is an independent unit or a part of a larger whole and whether all organizational responsibilities are handled by the senior theatre program. Chapter Five includes information on space and equipment for the office. Chapter Six describes marketing tasks handled by the office. This chapter focuses on establishing the work systems in a fully supportive office.

Planning and Organizing

For the creative endeavors of the theatre to flourish in the most conducive atmosphere, the support work of the office needs organization and structure. Although new products, skills, ideas, and procedures will come as an ongoing process, careful planning of the details of the work involved is always important.

Begin the organization of the office work by making a master list of areas to be handled or overseen. This list will be taken from the long- and short-range planning of the theatre and the continuing organizational obligations to be minded. Break down the master list into specific goals under each heading and continue to break these goals down into specific tasks. Place important dates and deadlines in a master calendar and then add specific goals and tasks to the calendar so that the deadlines can be met. Once this planning is complete, you can write job descriptions for the staff and volunteers and make equipment and general supply lists. An example of this procedure is included in Chapter Six with a marketing plan.

A master list for the office might contain the following:

1. productions/tours
2. workshops
3. marketing
4. fund-raising
5. accounting/bookkeeping
6. records/reports
7. volunteer coordination
8. business pertaining to board of directors
9. socials/special events
10. space and equipment management

Some of these areas may be very large and should be broken down into several parts before specific goals and tasks are listed. In order to make such a list more manageable, routine tasks can be delegated as daily, weekly, monthly, quarterly, and annual projects. The special projects and campaigns for the year can be placed into the calendar, taking these routine tasks into consideration.

Once the tasks are specified, they can be assigned to staff members and volunteers. Part-time or periodic office help can be better coordinated, since scheduling of tasks can be more predictable with this organization.

This master list of office work, broken down into goals and tasks, can be the basis for an office manual in which instructions and information are added to the basic tasks. This can give workers a reference guide and will make training of staff and volunteers a much simplified process.

Communications

Although a telephone and a typewriter were the only two basic pieces of equipment for The Seasoned Performers office when it started and these are still essentials for much of the communications we do, the world has moved to the point where a computer system is almost a necessity for an office supporting a program of significant size. Putting the world at the fingertips and saving time and energy, computers can be especially advantageous for an office using senior adult staff or volunteers.

A computer with a system of word-processing, spreadsheet, and database potential is a simple beginning point. This will handle basic correspondence, grant proposals and other text files, record keeping, statistics, budgets and financial reports, the basic mailing lists, and other useful data. It can be used to bring various information together for reports. Communications systems—Internet, fax, e-mail—can be added to the computer as well as a desktop publishing and design program, all very useful technology for theatre offices. Plan time and budget for necessary training as new programs or systems are added.

Certain settings can be customized for computer users to compensate for slightly slowed reflexes. For instance, some senior adults have trouble clicking the mouse button fast enough to double click objects on the screen. Most computer operating systems allow you to adjust this double click speed on a mouse control panel. Larger monitors make text on the screen bigger and may be a good choice for older workers.

In an office that supports senior adult activities, the telephone will be well used. It is wise to avoid an extremely complicated telephone system, and the addition of an amplifier for the handset will be helpful for use by those with any hearing impairment. Remember that printed communications should be made easy to read with high contrast and slightly larger print.

The office will be the hub of communications for all production work, volunteer organization, ticket sales and tour coordination, fund-raising, public relations, planning, and general business. It will be necessary that information in all areas be organized and accurate. Chapter Six describes the many communications responsibilities that an office may handle for marketing the theatre.

Record Keeping

Good record keeping reflects good general management of a theatre and can help justify your plans and needs. The types of records required by umbrella organizations, funding agencies, and governments will, to a great extent, dictate the types of information and statistics kept by the office. Special documentation may be required for some of these records. It will save time in the long run to tailor some record keeping to the requirements of standard reports and forms of granting agencies and other support organizations. There are also advantages to keeping certain other records that will give you valuable information for future growth and planning and for marketing and fund-raising purposes. The following general records are suggested:

1. Bookkeeping—Legalities and standard methods will regulate this system. From these records, produce a simplified list of income with sources and expenses with categories.
2. Documentation—Copies of invoices, canceled checks, receipts, and other items are required by some supporting agencies and will serve as proof of transactions.
3. Performances, workshops, and special events— Include the number of events and financial information for each project.
4. Sites served—Divide these into urban, suburban, and rural, and track the cities, counties, and states.
5. Audience—Record the numbers including senior adults, handicapped, students, and minorities. Collect a list of potential audience members and groups to add to the mailing list.
6. Participants/volunteers—Keep personal information including address, telephone number, special health concerns, and number of hours donated for work.
7. Marketing—Record the number of mailers and press releases sent, media contacted and results, records of other marketing, and copies of all printed publicity.
8. Evaluation sheets and notes—Maintain a current file from audience, participants, and supporters. Keep especially memorable quotes for marketing purposes.
9. Information on other senior adult services, especially senior arts programs—These details can help with future planning and possible joint projects.
10. Information on funding agencies, corporations, other potential sources—Successful grant proposals and other fund-raising can be based on your knowledge.

11. History of your theatre program—Include photographs, articles, flyers, statistics, etc. for each production, workshop, or other programming.
12. General correspondence—Keep as much as possible on computer disks for ease of storage and accessing for reference.
13. Equipment service records and inventory—Storing the inventory on a computer disk makes it especially easy to update.

Reports based on the various statistics the office keeps can give a picture of where the theatre stands in relation to programming and service, funding and budgets, and marketing goals. It will be helpful to produce these reports on a monthly, quarterly, and annual basis as well as per show or project. Once these systems are set up, it will be a routine and quick job to produce the reports. These will be used in making post-project reports for granting agencies and other supporting entities, for projecting budgets, in writing grant proposals for the future, and in creating annual reports for your board.

Staff

Once planning and organizing of the office work is done, the staff size can be considered. Budgets and scope of programming will dictate whether full- or part-time staff is needed and whether paid or volunteer help will be used. Be realistic in pairing workload and staff so that jobs can be done well and deadlines met without overwhelming the personnel. Everything that the theatre does will be affected by the quality of the office support.

When staffs are necessarily small, as they often are in theatre, there is opportunity for multiple job assignments. The clerical assistant may also take on the responsibility of tour management or ticket sales supervision, for instance. However managed, the staff responsibilities should be clearly defined. Use the master plan to clarify job assignments.

Senior adult theatres have both a duty and a grand opportunity to rely on the skills and dedication of an older workforce in all areas. It may be beneficial to design some office jobs that would be especially attractive to retired persons. This may involve shorter and flexible hours and sharing of responsibilities.

. . .

Although the offices of senior adult theatres will be as varied as the many individual theatres themselves, the fact remains that much will depend on the efficient and accurate methods used there. The nature of senior adult theatre can bring about unexpected problems. The office must be prepared to handle unplanned events as well as the planned with its systems of communications and information. It is an important element in the makeup of a strong program and can be instrumental in the longevity of a senior adult theatre.

An Encouraging Word

Just as children's theatre has done, senior adult theatre is making an indelible mark on the world. There is a real demand for theatre focusing on the special needs of the older population, whatever shape or form an individual theatre may take.

Although I've tried to focus on the nuts and bolts of starting and running a senior adult theatre, there is also an emotional commitment that must be made. Senior theatre can be a roller coaster ride of pride and disappointment, joy and sorrow. At times it can be smooth sailing. For me, it has been overall a positive and deeply satisfying journey as I've watched something wonderful develop.

Hopefully, the lessons contained in this book will help you avoid or manage some of the problems. But even the best-run senior theatre will face difficult moments. These are the times when you will learn the most valuable lessons. And at these times you may share the most heart-warming support of some of your older associates who will recognize your commitment and caring. They will teach you that you shouldn't take this theatre business too seriously. Set up your theatre to be fun even as you work toward fulfilling your vision.

Use the information, advice, and guidelines as you will—or do it your own way. The reward is in the trying—and the staying. It may be a roller coaster, but enjoy the ride. And . . . break a leg!

Appendix I

One-Act Plays Commissioned by The Seasoned Performers

This listing includes plays that may be of interest to other groups. Individual playwrights hold the copyrights to these plays and may be contacted for further information.

- *Bloomers, Bubblegum, and Brown Paper Bags* or *Why Didn't I Think of That?* by Betty Pewitt and Jean Pierce—Mother of Invention takes various characters on tours through vignettes showing how some ordinary but helpful items were invented. (40 minutes, comedy, educational, cast: 1m and 5f, or 6f, may use more individuals in cast.)
- *Fine Feathered Friends and the Rara Avis* by Betty Pewitt and Jean Pierce—Four longtime friends go on a birding expedition and find a few mysterious surprises. (40 minutes, comedy, adventure, cast: 4f.)
- *Rosa and the Rhinestone Star* by Betty Pewitt and Jean Pierce—A group of senior adults goes on a bus trip to Nashville. The bus breaks down and Rosa, the "quiet" one, saves the day with a pair of panty hose. (25 minutes, comedy/adventure, cast: 5f, one silent male or a mannequin may be used.)
- *The New Doctor* by Betty Pewitt—Two sisters deal with the trauma of having to find a new doctor when their lifelong physician retires. (15 minutes, comedy, cast: 1m and 3f, or 4f.)

Betty Pewitt
104 Club Village Drive
Birmingham, AL 35213
(205) 870-5470
Jean Pierce
(205) 879-3264

- *The China Pig* by Alan Litsey—Set in a historical museum in a small California town, an eccentric and charming mix of characters gather to help the community and try to connect with each other. (15 minutes, comedy/drama, cast: 1m and 4f, or 5f.)

Alan Litsey
Birmingham Southern College
900 Arkadelphia Road
Box 549026
Department of Theatre
Birmingham, AL 35254
(205) 226-4788
e-mail: *alitsey@bsc.edu*

- *Is This Funny, or What?* by Dick Deason and Martha Haarbauer—Celebrates and parodies the history of American performance comedy since Vaudeville. (40 minutes, comedy revue, cast: 6–16 individuals, can use up to 5m and 11f or all female, one silent role.)
- *Beyond Happily Ever After* by Martha Haarbauer—Cinderella, the Prince, and the Fairy Godmother cope with changes that come in their senior years. (15 minutes, comedy vignette, cast: 1m and 2f.)

Martha Haarbauer
2601 Highland Avenue, South
Birmingham, AL 35205
(205) 978-5095

(205) 822-6746

- *It's Perfectly True* by Randy Marsh—Set in a beauty
  shop in a small town, this modern southern comedy is
  based on a story of the same name by Hans Christian
  Anderson. (40 minutes, comedy, cast: 5f.)

Randy Marsh
502 Windsor Drive
Birmingham, AL 35209
(205) 879-8324

- *Jonas and the Wales* by Jeanmarie Collins and JoAnn
  Weatherly—Set in the attic of an old southern family
  home, the three Wale sisters and their first cousin
  meet to find a memento of their grandfather and find
  much more. (40 minutes, comedy, cast: 4f.)

JoAnn Weatherly
2134 Brookdale Lane
Birmingham, AL 35216
(205) 822-8045

- *Just Call Me Darling* by Bonnie Merryman—Two
  women in a retirement center decide to kidnap a
  newspaper woman to make their complaints public.
  (15 minutes, comedy, cast: 3f.)

Bonnie Merryman
1503 Timber Drive
Helena, AL 35080
(205) 916-6541
(205) 620-0543

- *On Becoming a Grandfather* by Dick Deason—A mono-
  logue for a mature man on the inexpressible feelings
  he has about his first grandchild. (10 minutes, serious
  comedy, cast: 1m.)

Dick Deason
510 Villa Esta Lane
Birmingham, AL 35214–3117

- *Suspicion* by Lee Eric Shackleford—Four longtime
  friends begin to suspect each other of doing wrong
  when something is missing from their gymnasium
  locker. (35 minutes, comedy/mystery, cast: 4f.)

Lee Eric Shackleford
PO Box 55704
Birmingham, AL 35255
(205) 621-5169
e-mail: *leeshack@mindspring.com*

- *Wordplay* by Barbara Sloan—A group of amateur
  actors rehearses its play about how some common
  expressions originated. (40 minutes, comedy, educational, cast: 1m and 5f, or 6f, one silent role.)

Barbara Sloan
1429 Panorama Drive
Birmingham, AL 35216
e-mail: *bjsloan@samford.edu*

Appendix II

Resources

General

Administration on Aging
330 Independence Avenue, SW
Washington, D.C. 20201
(800) 677-1116
(202) 619-7501
FAX: (202) 260-1012
e-mail: *aoainfo@aoa.gov*
Web site: *www.aoa.gov*

Age Exchange Reminiscence Centre
11 Blackheath Village
London SE3 9LA
United Kingdom
Tel: 011-44-181-318-9105
FAX: 011-44-0181-318-0600
e-mail: *Age-Exchange@lewisham.gov.uk*
Web site: *www.age-exchange.org.uk*

American Association of Retired Persons (AARP)
601 E Street, NW
Washington, D.C. 20049
(800) 424-3410
Web site: *www.aarp.org*

The National Council on the Aging, Inc.
409 Third Street SW
Washington, D.C. 20024
(202) 479-1200
FAX: (202) 479-0735
e-mail: *info@ncoa.org*
Web site: *www.ncoa.org*

National Endowment for the Arts
Nancy Hanks Center
1100 Pennsylvania Avenue, NW
Washington, D.C. 20506–0001
(202) 682-5400
Web site: *www.arts.endow.gov*

Senior Theatre Connections
1236 NE Siskiyou Street
Portland, OR 97212
Web site: *www.seniortheatre.com*

Senior Theatre Research and Performance
Web site: *www.accad.ohio-state.edu/~jreilly/index.html*

Senior Resource
Web site: *www.seniorresource.com*

University of Nevada–Las Vegas
Department of Theatre Arts
Senior Adult Theatre Program
4505 S. Maryland Parkway
Box 455036
Las Vegas, NV 89154–5036

Publishers

ArtAge Publications
PO Box 12271
Portland, OR 97212–0271
(503) 249-1137
e-mail: *bonniev@teleport.com*
Web site: *www.seniortheatre.com*

Baker's Plays
100 Chauncy Street
Boston, MA 02111
(617) 482-1280
FAX: (617) 482-7613
Web site: *www.bakersplays.com*

I. E. Clark Publications
PO Box 246
Schulenburg, TX 78956–0246
(409) 743-3232
FAX: (409) 743-4765
e-mail: *ieclark@cvtv.net*

Dramatists Play Service, Inc.
440 Park Avenue South
New York, NY 10016
(212) 683-8960
FAX: (212) 213-1539
e-mail: *postmaster@dramatists.com*
Web site: *www.dramatists.com*

Dramatic Publishing
311 Washington Street
Woodstock, IL 60098

(800) 448-7469
FAX: (800) 334-5302
Web site: *www.dramaticpublishing.com*

Heinemann
361 Hanover Street
Portsmouth, NH 03801–3912
(603) 431-7894
FAX: (603) 431-7840
Web site: *www.heinemann.com*

New Plays Inc.
PO Box 5074
Charlottesville, VA 22905

Pleasant Hill Press
473 Peacock Boulevard
Lafayette, CA 94549
(925) 284-7342

Thornapple Publishing Co.
7180 Thornapple River Road
PO Box 256
Ada, MI 49301
(616) 676-1583

Samuel French, Inc.
45 West 25th Street–Dept. W
New York, NY 10010
(212) 206-8990
FAX: (212) 206-1429

Web site: *www.samuelfrench.com*

Senior Adult Theatres Profiled

Curtain Time Retirement Vignettes
PO Box 256
Ada, MI 49301

Extended Run Players
University of the Incarnate Word
4301 Broadway
San Antonio, TX 78209

Footsteps of the Elders
693 Yaronia Drive
Columbus, OH 43214–3138

Kirkwood Accomplished Thespian Society
Kirkwood By The River Retirement Community
3605 Ratliff Road
Birmingham, AL 35210

The Merry Clements Players
1580 Yarrow Street
Lakewood, CO 80215

The Ripe and Ready Players
Senior Neighbors
10th and Newby Streets
Chattanooga, TN 37402

The Seasoned Performers
2601 Highland Avenue South
Birmingham, AL 35205

Slightly Older Adult Players (SOAP)
Fort Collins Senior Center
1200 Raintree
Fort Collins, CO 80526

Stagebridge
2501 Harrison Street
Oakland, CA 94612
Web site: *www.stagebridge.org*

Author

Suzanne Carter
Senior Neighbors
10th and Newby Streets
Chattanooga, TN 37402
e-mail: *emmaparis@aol.com*

Appendix III

Sample Grant Proposal Narrative and Response to Evaluation Criteria

The following narratives are two sections of a Project Assistance Program grant proposal to the Alabama State Council on the Arts, the official state agency for the support and development of the arts in Alabama. Similar state agencies exist in every state. Be sure to obtain current application forms and guidelines before applying.

The form used in this example requested applicant information, a detailed request profile, the activity narrative (printed here), qualifications of personnel involved in the project, an organizational profile, response to the evaluation criteria (printed here), projected budget with income and expenses specified, grant history of the applicant organization, assurances signed by authorizing officials, and supplemental information describing accomplishments of past projects and use of grant funds. Applicants were asked to inform the council of intent to apply in advance of the deadline and to submit an original and two copies of the current application form with any supporting materials by the deadline.

Activity Narrative

This application is for funds which would enable The Seasoned Performers to commission a script for older adult actors which will be appropriate to audiences of various ages, and to conduct an initial two-month [dates] tour of a production of the script performed by senior adult actors. The play will later continue its tour for another two months in the fall [dates].

The project provides for a collaboration between the Performers and directors, a professional writer, and an education consultant to assure good theatrical and educational quality. It will tour to groups in schools, churches, retirement facilities, community centers, and libraries. A study guide will be developed for use by teachers in their classrooms. The play will tour to sixty-five sites. The project also provides for an additional position of a guest Artistic Director.

The goals of this project are (1) to provide an opportunity especially for senior adults to participate in a high-grade theatrical production, (2) to provide The Seasoned Performers with a new script that would add variety to the program for both performers and audiences, (3) to bring a live theatrical experience to a variety of audiences, largely constituencies of senior adults and young students, including some underserved groups and areas, and (4) to develop the quality and educational potential of the overall program.

Response to Evaluation Criteria

1. *Description of potential artistic quality of project, including quantitative information:*

    Since 1984 the quality of the productions of The Seasoned Performers has consistently grown—with material, technical potential, abilities of the performers, and experience of the directors. Some of the performers have years of previous experience in theatre, many have been touring with the Performers for up to ten years, while others are getting experience in the training workshops and reading programs with the Performers. Other professionals, including a guest artistic director, are now involved in the process of creating the productions. The artistic quality of recent productions has been excellent. Since 1986 The Seasoned Performers has commissioned and produced the work of a dozen professional Alabama writers. [Other personnel qualifications were specified in another section.]

2. *General Narrative Profile of the project's history, describing how it will serve the community:*

There is an ever-growing population of older adults who are still active and who wish to be mentally stimulated by the ideas and entertainment that theatre can bring. These older adults have special needs and considerations both as participants in the arts and as audience members. The touring productions of The Seasoned Performers make an effort to address those needs and considerations while presenting a theatrical piece with high artistic quality. As the program has developed its style and focus over The Seasoned Performers' fifteen-year history, the most efficient and effective means has evolved to the present project format. Developing material for and by older adults (while entertaining and enlightening students and audiences of all ages) is a unique goal of this project, as is reaching audiences in nontheatrical community sites.

3. *Description of planned outreach efforts to expand public awareness and involvement in the arts, and how the project would benefit underserved geographic areas or population groups:*

This project targets groups of older and younger audiences, as well as general audiences, in schools, retirement facilities, churches and community centers, and libraries. Activities directors of retirement facilities and other community groups and enrichment teachers and principals in schools are contacted to assist in scheduling the tour. Direct mailings, personal contacts, press releases in major newspapers, television, and radio stations, and in special publications for older adults and for teachers will be used for publicity. Human interest stories will be offered to the media. This production will be taken to sixty-five sites in north/central Alabama, where small and large groups meet. A special effort is made to include underserved populations in rural and inner-city areas, and low economic populations with "free" or "sponsored" performances. The Seasoned Performers' tours serve an average annual audience of 6,000—50% senior adults, 40% students, including 25%–30% minority and 19% handicapped members. Of the sixty-five total performances, 78% are for senior adult groups and 20% are either donated or underwritten so that they can be free to certain audiences, and 11% are in rural areas.

4. *Description of overall planning efforts reflecting broad-based participation by members of the organization and community, including methods to be used to evaluate the effectiveness of the project:*

The Seasoned Performers continues its collaborative effort with Performers and directors, the writer, and an education consultant working together from the beginning and throughout the project. A script is planned for senior adult actors with specific guidelines to fit audiences of various ages and providing elements of educational value for students. The project director oversees fund-raising efforts for the project with assistance from the Advisory Committee and administrators of the Jefferson County Council on Aging and the Jefferson County Office of Senior Citizens Services. Other professionals in the areas of aging and education are consulted and are active in scheduling the tour. The production will be constantly reviewed by the collaborative team during the creative process and the tour. An audience profile will be kept and audience response will be recorded as the show tours. A survey questionnaire rating different aspects of the production will be filled out by the contact person for each group and returned to the Performers' office.

5. *Issues reflecting the need for financial support and any special considerations not otherwise addressed:*

Sixty-four percent of the operating budget, including all of the production expenses of the touring show must be raised through donations, grants, performance charges, and special fund-raising projects. A project of this quality involving professional artists and touring expenses would not be possible without the assistance requested. Also, with the assistance, charges can be kept low for all our audiences of senior adults and children, and fee waivers can be made so that economically disadvantaged groups can be served.

Appendix IV

Sample Bylaws of a Nonprofit Senior Adult Theatre

Printed by permission of the SOAP Troupe, the following is a reproduction of bylaws that are for a uniquely structured senior adult theatre and is intended as an example, not necessarily as a model. Some aspects, such as the membership and dues requirements, may be unusual for many senior adult theatres.

Bylaws of the SOAP Troupe

Article I
The name of this organization shall be THE SOAP TROUPE. The term SOAP in the name is an acronym for the words "Slightly Older Adult Players."

Article II—Objectives and Policies
Section A. Objectives
1. To furnish a vehicle to enable members to take part in live stage productions and other theatrical endeavors.
2. To provide opportunities for members to participate in other types of theatrical and/or dramatic activities such as musicals, play reading, comedy, poetry reading, skit presentation, charades, oral interpretation, etc.

Section B. Policies
1. There will be at least one live play or musical of at least one act in length produced each year; there will

not be any limit to the number of such productions planned and presented, so long as they are approved by a vote of the membership. Other theatrically related activities shall be conducted as the membership wishes.

2. The organization shall be nonprofit.
3. The organization shall operate under the auspices of the City of Fort Collins Parks and Recreation Department, Older Adult Program. A staff member from the Older Adult Program, appointed by the Director of the Older Adult Program, shall be an ex officio member of the Board of Directors.

Article III—Membership

Section A. There shall be two classes of membership, Regular and Affiliate.

1. REGULAR MEMBERSHIP shall be limited to those persons who have reached their fiftieth birthday and who are deemed in good standing by the Board of Directors by virtue of being current in their annual dues to this organization and being bona fide members of the Senior Center Division of the Fort Collins Parks and Recreation Department. Regular members shall have full voting privileges at and of the organization's general meetings.
2. AFFILIATE MEMBERSHIP shall be granted to those persons who have been invited by the Board of Directors to become affiliated with this organization for the purpose of assisting in its goals, mission, and/or activities. This class of membership shall not be required to pay dues and will not have voting privileges. Age will have no bearing on this class of membership. Affiliate members will have a voice at general membership meetings only if recognized by the Chair.

Article IV—Dues

Section A. The annual dues of this organization shall be an amount established by the Board of Directors and ratified by the membership at the annual meeting. Such dues shall be due and payable at the annual meeting.

Section B. The Board of Directors may waive the dues requirement in hardship cases. Such waiver shall be held confidential.

Article V—Officers and Their Election

Section A. The officers of the organization shall be a President, a Vice President, a Secretary, and a Treasurer.

Section B. The officers shall be elected at the annual meeting to serve for one year. Election shall be by written ballot unless there is only one candidate for each office in which case voting may be done by voice.

Section C. Vacancies. A vacancy in office shall be filled by a special election held at a meeting called for that purpose following the announcement of the vacancy, with the exception of a vacancy in the office of President. In such case, the Vice President shall automatically become President and the Vice Presidency shall become vacant.

Article VI—Board of Directors

Section A. The officers elected at the annual meeting shall automatically become members of the Board of Directors upon their election; the retiring officers shall cease to be members of the Board as of that election.

Section B. Composition. The Board of Directors shall consist of eight (8) members as follows: The four elected officers—Three at-large members elected at the annual meeting to serve on the Board—One ex officio appointee from the city administration. Two of the at-large members shall be elected to serve a two-year term so that there will be a continuity of Board membership from year to year.

The ex officio member shall not have a vote in Board business but shall have a voice in Board proceedings.

Article VII—Duties of Officers

Section A. President. The President shall:

1. Preside at all meetings of the organization.
2. Appoint all standing committee chairs and other committees not provided for in these bylaws.
3. Conduct this office by the letter and spirit of these bylaws.
4. Perform any other reasonable duties within the framework of this organization as requested or directed by the Board of Directors.

Section B. Vice President. The Vice President shall:

1. Perform the President's duties whenever the President is unable to fulfill them; will be subject to the same mandates of the Presidency.
2. Attend all official meetings of the organization unless excused.
3. Perform other reasonable duties as requested by the President.
4. Chair the Publicity Committee.

Section C. Secretary. The secretary shall:

1. Attend all official meetings of the organization unless excused.
2. Record all official minutes of said meetings, maintain a file of such minutes, and turn over such file to any successor. Said minutes will be readily available for any review or audit by the President or his designee.
3. Preside at meetings when both the President and Vice President are absent.
4. Conduct any reasonable organizational business as requested by the President.
5. Be responsible for any correspondence required for carrying out the business of the organization.

6. In the absence of another appointed chair, chair the Audit Committee.

Section D. Treasurer. The Treasurer shall:

1. Attend all official meetings of the organization unless excused.
2. Receive and properly deposit all receipts of the organization and make proper accounting for such monies when requested by the President or the President's designee.
3. Keep such accounting records as necessary.
4. Keep the minutes of any official meetings in the absence of the Secretary.
5. Make a formal financial report to the membership at the annual meeting.
6. Be available for the conduct of an audit at any reasonable time as requested by the President and provide all accounting books as needed for a proper audit.
7. Be responsible for setting up and maintaining a proper bank account. Said bank account shall have at least three of the elected officers as signers for the account, with two of the three signatures required on all checks.
8. Conduct any reasonable organizational business as requested by the President.

Article VIII—Standing Committees

Section A. Executive Committee. Will consist of the four elected officers and the ex officio city staff member. Will meet whenever the President or other officer feels a meeting is needed.

Section B. Activities Committee.

1. The President will appoint the chair of this committee, who will recruit up to three other members to serve.
2. Will recommend the plays or other activities this organization will produce or conduct in the upcoming year and

report their selections to the Board of Directors for their approval no later than the last of November of each year.

3. Shall serve at the pleasure of the Board of Directors. Members of this committee may be removed or replaced as the Board sees fit.

Section C. Publicity Committee.

1. This committee will be chaired by the Vice President, who will recruit up to three other members to serve.

2. Will be responsible for providing publicity or delegating others to provide publicity for the general activities of the organization and for specific productions and activities.

3. Shall serve at the pleasure of the Board of Directors. Members of this committee may be removed or replaced as the Board sees fit.

Section D. Audit Committee.

1. The chair of this committee will be appointed by the President; in the event that another chair cannot be found, the Secretary will assume the chairmanship. The chair will recruit two other persons to serve, one from outside the organization who has auditing or accounting experience.

2. Each year prior to the annual meeting this committee will examine the financial records and prepare a report to be presented at the annual meeting.

3. Shall serve at the pleasure of the Board of Directors. Members of this committee may be removed or replaced as the Board sees fit.

Section E. Nominating Committee.

1. Three members will be elected to the Nominating Committee at the November meeting.

2. The chair of the committee will be selected from within the committee.

3. All SOAP Troupe members will be polled.

4. A slate of officers will be presented by the committee at the annual meeting.

Article IX—Meetings and Quorums

1. The annual meeting shall be called by the Board of Directors sometime during the month of January each year. A written notice of this meeting will be given both classes of membership no later than seven days before the annual meeting is to take place.

2. The purposes of this meeting will be to: (1) elect officers and at-large Board members, (2) ratify the annual dues structure for the coming year and approve the calendar of events insofar as this is possible, and (3) conduct any other business as deemed necessary by the Board.

3. An agenda will be generated by the elected officials for each general meeting, and the order of business will be set by the President. A copy of this agenda will be given to each REGULAR and AFFILIATE member, and to the ex officio member, who are in attendance.

4. Other general meetings may be scheduled as directed by the President or the Board of Directors, provided all members are notified of said meeting by telephone or in writing at least seven days prior to said meeting.

5. The Board of Directors may have as many Board meetings as they deem necessary to conduct the business of this organization. There will be no restrictions as to the agenda of these meetings.

6. Executive Committee meetings will be called at the pleasure of the President.

7. Quorums. Ten percent of the REGULAR membership in good standing shall constitute a quorum at all annual and special general membership meetings.

Membership must be in attendance, with no written proxies being recognized for the purpose of fulfilling quorum requirements. At all Board of Directors meetings at least four of the seven elected officials must be present. At all Executive Committee meetings, at least three of the four members must be present.

Article X—Parliamentary Authority

Section A. Robert's Rules of Order, Newly Revised, shall apply on all questions of procedure and or parliamentary law not specified in these bylaws.

Section B. These bylaws may be amended under the following conditions and procedures:

1. The Board must furnish, in writing, at least seven days before any meeting where the bylaws will be discussed, to each REGULAR member in good standing, the article(s) to be proposed for change or modification, along with the reasons for such change and/or modification.
2. At least two-thirds of the voting members present must approve any and all changes or modifications.
3. The changes/modifications must be presented in one meeting, but will not be voted on until the next meeting.

Approved: October 2, 1991
Revised: March 21, 1995

Bibliography

Billig, N. 1993. *Growing Older and Wiser*. New York: Lexington Books.

Carter, S. *Making It Up As You Go Along*. Available through the author.

Fuller, T. W., ed. 1996. *Seniors Acting Up: Humorous New One-Act Plays and Skits for Older Adults*. Pleasant Hill, CA: Pleasant Hill Press.

Hopkins, B. R. 1989. *A Legal Guide to Starting and Managing a Nonprofit Organization*. New York: John Wiley & Son, Inc.

McDonough, A. 1994. *The Golden Stage: Dramatic Activities for Older Adults*. Dubuque, IA: Kendall/Hunt Publishing Co.

———. 1998. *The Golden Stage: Dramatic Activities for Older Adults Teacher's Guide*. 2d ed. Woodstock, IL: Dramatic Publishing Co.

———, ed. 1997. *New Monologues for Mature Actors*. Woodstock, IL: Dramatic Publishing Co.

———, ed. 1998. *Short Stuff: Ten- to Twenty-Minute Plays for Mature Actors*. Woodstock, IL: Dramatic Publishing Co.

———, ed. 1999. *A Grand Entrance: Scenes and Monologues for Mature Actors*. Woodstock, IL: Dramatic Publishing Co.

Redd, R. O. 1998. *21 Humorous, New Short Plays and Skits for Performing Grandparents*. Ada, MI: Thornapple Publishing Co.

Telander, M., F. Quinlan, and K. Verson. 1982. *Acting Up!* Chicago: Coach House Press, Inc.

Vorenberg, B. L. 1987. *New Plays for Mature Actors*. Morton Grove, IL: Coach House Press, Inc.

———. 1999. *Senior Theatre Connections*. Portland, OR: ArtAge Publications.

Wilder, R. 1996. *Come, Step into My Life*. Charlottesville, VA: New Plays Inc.